"Father Bill Bausch has again made a ι
his other books, *The Hands-On Parish* cu...... uuι uι a ιιιe lived
where it all happens. No ivory tower approach here....There is
theory; there is theological reflection; there is sound speculation
about today's scene; there is a keen sense of history; there is familiarity with the literature. But a sharp, insightful 'common sense'
kind of mind wrestles with all of it. Thus, the book is interlaced
with practical advice and creative suggestions for making your
parish a 'hands on' one. You will hear yourself saying again and
again, 'What a great idea!'"

The Rev. Frank McNulty
Pastor, Our Lady of the Blessed Sacrament Parish
Roseland, N.J.

"Already one in twenty American parishes is without a priest,
and for the foreseeable future things will only get worse. Is all
this news as bad as it seems? Not necessarily, according to Father William J. Bausch, who has been charting parish develop-
ments in the United States for many years. In fact, he argues
that what seems to many to be a crisis can instead be turned
into an opportunity—one in which the laity regains much of
the ministry that it held historically and to which it has been
summoned again by the Second Vatican Council. Bausch makes
this and many other intriguing points in *The Hands-On Parish*. I
say 'intriguing' because Bausch succeeds in pulling together a
number of approaches in one volume.

Gerald M. Costello
U.S. Catholic

"Part parish manual, part anecdotal daybook, part Catholic history, part communications guide, part marketing handbook,
part resource compendium, the book is a pocket organizer for
congregational life. It is a work to be read, to be studied, to be
referred to, in short a work to keep one's hands on. Fr.
Bausch's style is eclectic, allusive, chatty, and quite encycloped-
ic. It seems ready to go off in any direction at any time. On
any given page he might tell a little parish story, refer to twentieth-century history, quote a contemporary American journalist
or a Desert Father or both, interpret the latest statistics, and explain a graphic or two!"

Paul Matthew St. Pierre
British Columbia Catholic

"As in his other books about parish life, Father Bausch writes from personal experience in his own parish and from the stories he has heard in his travels as speaker and workshop presenter around the country. He writes clearly and with enthusiasm about real people solving real problems we have all faced. He offers a new agenda for parishes for the '90s and then gives more than 100 practical ideas for building a strong community (I counted 117)."

Pat Durbin
Catholic Times

"William Bausch continues to offer pastorally sound, theologically solid, and eminently practical ideas on parish life. The book is built on the premise that holiness is open to everyone, not just vowed or ordained people....Bausch's gift is to be able to communicate fundamental concepts with vivid and familiar language. Practical examples of community building abound."

Maureen Gallagher
Archbishop's Delegate for Parishes
Archdiocese of Milwaukee

"What can a Protestant minister learn from William Bausch's reflections on fifteen years as a parish priest? I discovered that Bausch has the pastoral wisdom of Robert Hudnut, the cultural sensitivity of Lyle Schaller, the promotional and communication skills of Robert Schuller and the missionary zeal of Frank Tillapaugh. Bausch provides an excellent description of a theology of the laity and a priesthood of all believers....Bausch's book is a delightful blend of grassroots theology and here's-how-*we*-did-it stories."

John E. Stanley
Christian Ministry

"The Hands-On Parish offers a wide variety of ideas for many persons; indeed, a parish trying to use everything in the book would be abuzz with activity. But this isn't an ivory-tower think piece; it's pastorally sound, theologically solid, with eminently practical ideas for parishes.

Edward O'Meara
The Catholic Sentinel

William J. Bausch

T·H·E
HANDS-ON
PARISH

*Reflections and Suggestions
for Fostering Community*

TWENTY-THIRD PUBLICATIONS
Mystic, Connecticut

Dedication

For "Doctor," O'B, Eddie and others,
mentored, mentors
and for J.C.R.,
Macbeth, Act III 1, 108

Third printing 1994

Twenty-Third Publications
185 Willow Street
P.O. Box 180
Mystic, CT 06355
(203) 536-2611
800-321-0411

ISBN 0-89622-401-5
Library of Congress Catalog Card Number 89-51416

Preface

Three reasons prompted this book. The first is the special interest of those who took the "hands-on" parish workshops with me. The advertised emphasis of these workshops was on the practical. The actual workshop was even more demanding of the practical than I had anticipated. In other words, people wanted some theory and an overview of where parishes might be going in the next decade or so, but even more they wanted concrete examples that flowed from the theory. They wanted ideas to build community, to make their parishes come alive. Their questions and needs are reflected in this book. Second, over the years, a constant stream of letters have asked the same questions: how do you do this, what can we do here, and, most of all, can you give us some ideas? Their questions and needs are also reflected in this book. Third, after completing what I called a trilogy about parish life and ministry (*The Christian Parish; Ministry: Traditions, Transitions, Tensions;* and *Take Heart, Father*—all Twenty-Third Publications), there were still important, or at least useful, things to say about parish ministry.

There are about one hundred ideas that will encourage a "hands-on" parish experience. I'm not going to scream, as do the silly blurbs, "and much, much more!" No, just about a hundred and that will do nicely. In fact, to save some readers from what might be a burden of reading the whole text when all they are looking for is a "bottom line," and for those who want easy visual sighting, I have marked each of the ideas with a ❑ sign. This allows people to skip all the rest or check off the appealing ideas. Of course, I think that some or most of "all the rest" of the book is quite, nay, even critically, important, but, out of pastoral mercy, I have specifically marked off the ideas.

A further hint for the reader: you will notice that the book, like Caesar's Gaul, is divided into three parts. Part One, "The New Agenda," containing Chapters 1 to 4, is the theory, the directions I feel the parish should be going, the agenda it should be considering, the matters that pastoral ministers should be seriously discussing. Skip it if you want to. But you shouldn't want to. Part Two, "Hands On," Chapters 5 to 15, contains most of the practical "hands-on" ideas and is filled with those little boxes (❑). Part Three, "Hands Off," containing the last two chapters and an afterword, returns to some theoretical ruminations.

It should be taken for granted that everything in the book reflects a limited view and experience. Some things are beyond both my view and experience, and those who know such have every right to look with question or even disdain at what is presented here. I remember recently attending a funeral at a wonderful parish in Brooklyn, the Redemptorist basilica of Our Lady of Perpetual Help. Although the neighborhood was lined with double-parked and stripped cars, and with grafitti sprayed everywhere, the church and its property were lovely and the church building remains imposing. They seem to have it all together in what must be a wholly different atmosphere from what I know. I noticed that their bulletin advertises a night of recollection for "all parishioners engaged in parish ministry: eucharistic ministers, lectors, ushers, catechists, security guards...." It's that last category that gets me and tells me how limited and restricted my world is. I have no experience of commissioning parish security guards.

But I do have enough experience to know that I must say something about the tone of the book. It's basically a book of ideas, ideas more to be seen, joined in and savored than read. However, since we *are* dealing with the printed page rather than the experience, I have to take something of an "expert" approach in writing this book: presenting information, attitudes, ideas—and opinions—with confidence and self-assurance. Am I that confident, that self-assured? Not really. Far from it. Like most others, I try. I roll with the punches, savor the successes, reflect on the failures, and look nervously out of the corner of my eye at someone who's doing it better and exclaim to myself, "God, why didn't I think of that!" I have a lot to learn.

Nevertheless, if I must still learn from so many, there is also much I have learned that I can teach. I am grateful for my experience of church in a particular time, space, and place, dimensions in my life that surely must resonate with those of many, many others. Such similarities and common ground entitle me to share. This book is the sharing.

Contents

PART ONE

The New Agenda

CHAPTER 1

Marketplace Revolution

In the mid-1980s, articles and workshops began to appear on a novel subject: marketplace spirituality. "Marketplace" was a loaded adjective. It was meant to indicate that a considerable shift had taken place in the Catholic consciousness. That shift proclaimed this: no longer were matters of holiness to be confined to esoteric convents, monasteries, and the retired life. Rather, holiness (with all its implications of mission and witnessing) was the very stuff and substance of all those out there beyond the walls, all those not ordained or solemnly consecrated to religious life, all those "nine-to-five" workers, all those homemaking, entertaining, playing, and loving human beings smack in the middle of life's swirl, noise, and activity.

All of a sudden the Spirit, who always blows where it will anyway, was openly acknowledged as blowing in the most mundane places and not just in the official "consecrated" spots. What caused this shift? Basically, there were two reasons for it, and that's what we're going to explore here—with serious implications both for the parish and parish ministers.

The first reason for this movement from monastic to marketplace spirituality is Vatican II.[1] We might remember that Vatican II spoke in several places of the nature of the church—especially in Chapters 4 and 5 of the *Dogmatic Constitution on the Church*—in such a way that it made a major shift in the church's self-understanding and existence. And what it said, at one stroke, removed centuries-old underpinnings for an inherited, elitist, hierarchical understanding of the Christian vocation. Undermined forever was the notion that the mission of the church was essentially a clerical preserve. No, the call in God's church clearly and unequivocally was to *universal* holiness.

This means that everybody is equally called to holiness and to mission. There was to be no clerical-lay split with the clergy leading and the laity following. There was to be no special active mission for priests and religious and a passive mission for the laity. No, the whole People of God was called to be church, to be holy, to sanctify this world. Therefore, the foundation of this calling was not ordination or religious vows, but baptism. Through baptism, there was one overriding mission for all but, of course, with a variety of gifts to help accomplish that mission. Being church was to be a communal enterprise. It was now to be an "age of the laity" or better, the age of the whole church and the old metaphors were revived: the People of God, the vine and the branches, the Mystical Body of Christ. A communal, concerted effort was called for, drawn from the same identical source: Jesus Christ—yesterday, today, and forever.

This has really been revolutionary and has caught us off guard both theologically and emotionally. The image of the church most of us carry around is that of the pyramid, and not just the pyramid as symbol of the governing or teaching church, but, more influentially on our everyday lives, a symbol of the way of salvation. For most people, this means that, starting from the pinnacle of full-time church work, everything seems to devolve in descending order of unworthiness, if not pollution, as far as holiness and mission go. If you made time and were devout, you would squeeze in some spirituality on Sunday or the annual mission, but never in the real world. As a kid, I remember that the most we could hope for was that, when our time came, we could sneak into purgatory with a scorched rump. Even the retreats for the laity gave this message by focusing mainly on prayer and the sacraments and seldom, if ever, on the gifts of the people for public witness and service. The equation came down to this: churchy activity= heightened spirituality; worldly activity= danger.

The result is that we have never developed a theology of work (efforts are being made now) or a spirituality of the marketplace, an understanding of God planted where-you-are, a sense of calling and mission, of co-creation. Actually, this is surprising because our roots show us an almost exclusive "lay" vocation. Some people were indeed called to follow Jesus, but most of those New Testament people were grounded—and remained grounded—in their world. Think, for example, of Zacchaeus, Simon's mother-in-law, the centurion, Jairus and his daughter, the Jericho blind man, the widow (of the mite fame), the woman with the hemorrhage, even Martha, Mary, and Lazarus. All were sent back or remained where they were with regenerated spirit and bodies. Perhaps the clearest instance of this is the woman at the well. We remember her only as the conniver who had five husbands. We don't always remember that she was sent back to her village and stayed to evangelize her neighbors and was the first to call Jesus "Savior."

Paul's lists of those strange Greek and Latin names—Pricilla and Aquila, Straphina and his wife, Trophosa, Andronicus and his wife, Julia, Nerius and his sister, Hermes and his brother, Rufus and his mother, Urban, Cornelius, Mary, Dorcas, Aristoplus, Narcissus, Stephanus—all testify that for every Barnabas or Mark who joined the missionary band, most stayed home to be church where they were in the marketplace.

Nevertheless, for all this tradition, as the centuries rolled by four prejudices conspired to move the people not only into a passive position but also into a spiritually inferior one. It would take us too far afield to go into the historical reasons for them, but we can at least identify what those four prejudices are. These prejudices constitute severe obstacles to the ideal of Vatican II's universal call to holiness.

Prejudice 1: Holiness Is Only for Priests and Sisters. This, no doubt, has to do with the upheavals of the dark ages and the barbarian invasions following the apostolic and patristic ages when the clergy, usually more educated and settled, were forced to fill the vacuum left by the civil power and to try to keep together some semblance of civilization. In any case, through the hierarchical structure of the church, the eminence and power of position, and the vast and influential monastic movement, the clergy and religious became not only the spiritual leaders but also the spiritual models. Without meaning to, they became almost the exclusive models as well. Note that, when the church revised the liturgical calendar a few years ago, of the 177 saints kept in, some 172 were celibate priests or religious, and the remaining were widows. That sums it up. Name your three favorite saints. Whoever you thought of, the odds are overwhelming that your choices are all priests, monks, or nuns. It's not just a question of an institution canonizing institutional people—remember, even Thomas More was canonized because he died for the supremacy of the pope, not because he was a husband and a father. It's a question of bias. Where is the woman canonized simply because she was a good mother? Where is the man canonized simply because he did an honest day's work?

So this prejudice remains strong. "Pray for me, Father" is not just a sensible request (why not?) but an unconscious inequality that since Father deals with sacred things he is closer to God. The kidding that "someday, when the kids are gone, my husband's retired and the dog is dead, I'm going to join the convent," is another nod to where "real" and "professional" holiness lies. Holiness, in this view, is for priests and sisters. That's what they're paid for. Of course, it must be admitted that this can be a handy prejudice: it can give some persons an excuse for not pursuing their own potential; for others it offers a dandy opportunity for reverse humility: why bother? I'm not the stuff saints are made of. It's not my job to evangelize. I'm not a priest or sister. (Community sponsorship in processes like the R.C.I.A. is trying to reverse this.)

Prejudice 2: The World Is Evil. This is a powerful and ambivalent prejudice. The early Christians, you recall, were a minority in a hostile world. Their world was full of their equivalent of pornography, cruelty, revenge, exploitation, and shady business dealings. They were persecuted by members of their own tribe (fellow Jews) and later on by the Roman government. If you add to this minority-persecuted status, their notion that the world was coming to an end and Jesus was returning soon, then you can hardly blame them for not being in love with the "world," their code name for wicked forces. After all, the Johannine Jesus did remind them, "If the world hates you, keep in mind that it hated me first. If you belonged to the world, it would love you as its own. As it is, you do not belong to the world, but I have chosen you out of the world " (John 15: 18).[2]

We acquired an attitude of what John Courtney Murray called an "eschatological theology" (a theology concerning the last things) that proclaimed, "Let us turn from the illusory seductions of this world. Let us live in patient hope, uninvolved in a fallen world, waiting for salvation." So, if for moderns, life begins after 5 P.M., for generations past, life began after death. With this attitude, the world can hold nothing but danger for us. It is evil and therefore the average person—living and working and raising his or her family in the world—has a disadvantage. No holiness is possible, at least not without either heroic effort or a good bit of "detachment," creating a private enclave apart from the world. (This is the sort of attitude that in our day would lead Liberation Theology to ask, "Has the very proper concern of Roman Catholicism with the salvation after death resulted in an unbiblical depreciation of this world?")

The ambivalence comes in because the Bible speaks of creation as good. Remember the old refrain after each day's creation, "And God saw that it was good"? Still, on the other hand, that same Bible gives us (with every other ancient source) the story of the Fall. That story says that creation has been corrupted by evil and that we have been separated from an original unity that we are striving to get back.[3] The "eternal is somehow away from us, and we have to find some way to get back in touch with it."[4] So we struggle to get released from this "prison" of a world and this prison of a body. We "withdraw" from the world in an effort to "de-materialize" ourselves, for we know, with Wordsworth, that:

> The world is too much with us; late and soon,
> Getting and spending, we lay waste our powers:
> Little we see in Nature that is ours;
> We have given our hearts away, a sordid boon!

The world, in our tradition, is not "user friendly." It is at least a morally dangerous place. To the question, can holiness be found in an evil world, most Christians would answer a timid no. The only hope is in fleeing it. Very few could appreciate Merton's insight:

> I believe that [God] has called me freely, out of pure mercy to His love and salvation. That at the end, to which all is directed by His will, I shall see Him after I have put off my body in death and have risen together with Him to take up my body again. That at that Last Day all flesh shall see the salvation of God.

> What this means is that my faith is an eschatological faith, not merely a means of penetrating the Divine Presence, and dwelling in Him or serving Him here and now. Yet,

because my faith is eschatological, it is also contemplative, for I am *even here and now* in the established kingdom. I can even now 'see' something of the glory of that kingdom and praise Him who is King. I would be foolish then if I live blindly, putting all seeing off until some imagined fulfillment, for my present seeing is the beginning of a real and unimaginable fulfillment.[5]

In any case, Christians who could not "see" sacramentally, who could not see daily revelation, who could not see the beginnings of the kingdom in creation and everydayness, reacted. The first two centuries saw the willing martyrs and the next two after that saw the hermits and monks going off to the desert. A tendency was starting there. The positive side is the marvelous legacy of a deep spirituality that can only be found in flight from the world and honed in the desert. Reading books like Benedicta Ward's *The Sayings of the Desert Fathers*, for example, gives testimony to what we owe these spiritual forebears. Still there was a negative side, and that was to leave the impression that the desert is the *only* place holiness can be found. Starting in the sixth century, the great missionary activities brought the monks out of the monastery to evangelize the world and called them back home again to the monastery in the tenth century in the Clunaic reform. The positive side was the incredible and heroic spread of the faith. Most of us are catholic Christians because a Boniface or a Brendan or a Cyril and Methodius took the road of high adventure. But again, the negative side of the missionary effort was the hidden message that to officially witness to the faith, one had to be a cleric. Even the inventive novelty of the wandering mendicants, the Dominicans and Franciscans and the Ignatian "contemplation in action" focus offered the positive side of moving into the streets and byways to preach and its negative message that still only a monastic or semi-monastic community lifestyle qualified one for mission.

It wasn't until the seventeenth century that the breakthrough came. The one responsible was St. Francis de Sales. His groundbreaking book, *Introduction to a Devout Life,* is still in print, and its preface catches the new spirit:

> Almost all those who have hitherto written about devotion have been concerned with instructing persons wholly withdrawn from the world, or have at least taught a kind of devotion that leads to such complete retirement. My purpose is to instruct those who live in towns, within families, or at court, and by their state of life are obliged to live an ordinary life as to outward appearances. Frequently, on the pretext of some supposed impossibility, they will not even think of undertaking a devout life.

As Father Thomas Green says, "It has taken 2000 years for us to begin to grasp the truth that God is really with us in the most radical sense. We don't have to flee to the desert, or even withdraw to the monastery in order to find him. Nor do we have to dichotomize our lives into separate times for encountering God and for coping with the world. He is present in the world for those who have the eyes to see."[6]

We might also take note of this: For the first thousand years of Christianity all the leading theologians were bishops and monks. Naturally, they evolved a "theology of the prie-dieu," theology and spirituality done on its knees, producing wisdom. In the high Middle Ages with the rise of the universities, the clergy and religious evolved a "theology of the desk," producing knowledge. But not Everyman or Everywoman had input into such esoteric wisdom and knowledge or could dicipher such formal structures, so once more spirituality and its theological expressions were removed from everyday life and critique. It's only now that we see some change. Now with the sensitivities of the various liberation, feminist, and black insights, we are striving to produce a "theology of the Marketplace." And this time it is being done by all the People of God, all having a part in the dialogue. Even the professional theologians are admitting that:

> We need to develop some type of hermeneutic circle [a

way of interpreting the Good News] whereby we bring experience [of the everyday people] Scripture, tradition together, trying to prevent the absolutization of any one of these aspects.[7]

What all this is saying is that the world is not so evil that grace cannot abound, be discovered, experienced, and shared. It is also saying that the people doing all the discovering and experiencing must be heard. No longer can the axiom "the world is evil" prevent any member of the People of God from experiencing saving grace, wherever he or she is, or from being responsible for the mission of the church or from contributing that experience to, or challenging, the Tradition. The world, too, is an arena of faith.

St. Francis de Sales was indeed a pioneer in bringing to mind our accessibility to holiness and our need to witness without fleeing the world, but in fact the old prejudice held and still holds. The habit, honed over the centuries as we have seen, persists: let George do it, "George" being the local priest, sister, or monk. This habit is so ingrained that when Catholic Action finally came along at the beginning of this century it was described as the "participation of the laity in the mission of the hierarchy." Vatican II disclaims this and now insists:

The laity are in their own way made sharers in the priestly, prophetic, and kingly functions of Christ. They carry out their own part in the mission of the whole Christian people with respect to the church and the world....the laity by their very vocation, seek the kingdom of God by engaging in temporal affairs and by ordering them according to the plan of God.[8]

Prejudice 3: Lack of Spiritual Direction. Although, as we know, the clergy and religious have always had spiritual direction accessible to them, the laity has not. This was not due to any conscious exclusion; it was "just the way things were." Spiritual direction was considered a luxury for those who had time, not the preserve of the hard-working laborer. So this lack, in its subtle way, tended once more to underline spirituality as the preserve of the elite, not the right of the common man or woman.

Prejudice 4: Institutionalizing the First Three Prejudices. This is more than a smart-aleck remark. It's just a way of reminding ourselves that inequalities are built into the structures and laws of our church and that we must continue to struggle to find new language. Now, I don't mean to say that there aren't differences and a legitimate hierarchy. It's only a dangerous anarchism or a silly shucking of responsibility that wants to reduce all gifts and authority to a common "democratic" denominator as if there were no difference between the learned and the stupid, the teacher and the pupil, the master and the disciple, the gifted and the untalented, legitimate authority and the common citizen. Rather, it's a matter of how our own church language, law, and structure do not allow for legitimate authority to function in an honest, collaborative, and servant way, and, most of all, do not allow for real images of equality of all the People of God. Think about it. As a church we do have all that official hierarchial language and assumptions, but on the other hand, we also have all that official language of participation, invitation, and equality. And they clash. For example, Canon 208 in the newly Revised Code of Canon Law speaks of a "genuine equality of dignity and action among all Christ's faithful," but Canon 207, just before it, reminds us that "by divine institution, among Christ's faithful there are in the church sacred ministers, who in law are called clerics; the others are called lay people."

So what? Well, we know what the canons mean intellectually, *but* emotionally they do in fact convey the impression that there really is inequality all the way around. Those canons symbolize the truth that we have basically a two-tier church, with the laity the inferior part of the tier. We are told that we are partners in the church—we and the hierarchy—and the latter is in service to the former, but it doesn't usually come off that way. All our language, our codes, are simply (and perhaps unconsciously) geared to remind us of lay "inferior" status. Try this quotation:

> The "laity" are by definition non-people. They are "non-ordained"; inferior because they have not been "raised" to the priesthood. Priests who leave are "reduced" to the "lay" state. We have ministers and "lay" ministers, readers and "lay" readers, catechists and "lay" catechists, chaplains and "lay" chaplains, spiritual directors and "lay" spiritual directors, theologians and "lay" theologians! We speak of "lay" Christians and even "lay" people! It is difficult to avoid subordinating the sub-group, the one which has the qualifying adjective — i.e. "lay," to the main group—minister. The "unqualified" one becomes by usage, the "normal," "real" or "better"....
>
> We have a cluster of meanings associated with the word "lay" which indicate a *lack* of something...we are left with the "laity" themselves as somehow less and the ministry exercised by "laity" as something less complete and less authoritative than the ministry exercised by clergy.[9]

We should be aware of our prejudices in our very language and mental images, for they often leave the impression that some are more called than others. If the marketplace revolution is to move ahead, if the conventional wisdom that "holiness is for priests and sisters," "the world is evil," and "ordinary people don't need spiritual direction" are to be subverted, then we have to look behind the assumptions that allow these prejudices to live and flourish.

We said at the beginning that there were two causes that shift these prejudices around. If the first cause is that revolutionary universal call to holiness of Vatican II, the second cause is best expressed by saying, "The issue just won't go away." What issue? The issue of why people should be concerned at all about marketplace spirituality. And that issue, simply put, is that people *do* experience God in the world and they need the tools to get a handle on this experience, to discern it. Or, as Father John Shea puts it, what we do, how we play, and who we hang around with, that is, we the Workers, the Players, and the Lovers in this world, do experience God and want to know what to do about it.[10]

Look at the facts. Gallup's Princeton Research center in October 1988 reported that a third of Americans have had a "religious experience"—a "particularly powerful religious insight or awakening."

One-third of 1000 Catholics interviewed by phone for a 1986 study of religious practices and beliefs in the Archdiocese of Miami reported having "a deepening religious experience, one that has been a turning point." A majority of 100 church professionals surveyed in 1985 reported having a religious experience. A 1976 survey conducted by Dean Hoge reported that 48 percent of Catholic youths felt that a particular event or experience "changed their feelings about God and the church." Theology professor and author Lawrence Cunningham speaks of "peak" experiences as indicating the presence of God, such as:

- the exhilarating moment of pain-esctasy that many parents report at the moment of the birth of their child.
- The awful moment of clarity when an addicted person realizes simultaneously that his or her life is a shambles and that there is a compelling need to reach out for help.
- Those moments when prayer is not an exercise in rote recitation but a genuine reaching out to another.
- The moment of a deeply felt conviction that one is forgiven and loved.
- The overwhelming sense when, for an instant, we genuinely see the beauty of nature.

Because most people lack either a technical or churchy vocabulary—especially in secular America—they tend to report or describe such experiences in the common coin of storytelling. They don't use religious words like grace or salvation or epiphany. They just tell their stories, which carry between-the-lines revelation:

Several years ago a group of computer salesmen from Milwaukee went to a regional sales convention in Chicago. They assured their wives that they would be home in plenty of time for dinner. But with one thing or another the meeting ran overtime so the men had to race to the train station, tickets in hand. As they barged through the terminal, one man (the one telling this story) inadvertently knocked over a table supporting a basket of apples which a young lad was selling. Without stopping, they reached the train and boarded it with a sigh of relief—all but one. He paused, got in touch with his feelings, and experienced a twinge of compunction for the boy whose apple stand he had overturned. He quickly jumped off the train, waved good by to his buddies, and returned to the terminal. He was glad he did. The lad was blind.

The salesman gathered up the fallen apples and noticed that several of them were bruised. He reached into his wallet and said to the boy, "Here, please take this ten dollars for the damage I did. I hope it didn't spoil your day." As he started to run away to catch another train, the bewildered boy called after him, "Are you Jesus?" He stopped in his tracks. And he wondered.[11]

As often as this man tells this story, that often he is trying to discern its meaning and the call behind the meaning. It's a report of his religious experience. And it is just such stories and such storytellers, like us all, that won't let the God issue die and in fact demand to make sense of how and why this God is revealed in our everydayness. People *do* have religious experiences. They want to affirm and decipher these experiences and the built-in mandate and mission that is implicit in every call.

People need to detect the Real Presence if for no other reason that they find the Real Absence intolerable. Most people's lives are faith lives that need to be noticed, talked about, and legitimized. Listen to this homemaker and writer:

We live complicated lives as working people, as parents,

as community volunteers. There's not a lot of time for extra involvement. The invitation seems to be "Come and do work in the church as ministers and leaders." For many people, that's not possible. There's no time. Or there's no desire....The church is the place I go to worship. But my faith is what I live, what I believe. It influences all my actions and my relationships. It sustains people through crises. It's much more a personal than an institutional thing. When I talk about faith, I mean something different from being a minister of Communion, although that may be one way of expressing it.[12]

So now the lines are drawn and the challenges given. Being church, being church with a call and a mission, being church publicly, that is, with full-fledged membership and responsibility—all this is something new for many "rank and file" people. They must rehear the Good News: spirituality and mission are no longer the preserve of the professionals; all have been the given the universal call to holiness.

For the local parish and parish ministers, the implications of this call serve as a new agenda for the twenty-first century.

CHAPTER 2

New Agenda
Part 1

As the consciousness of the universal call to holiness takes hold, I can see five areas of challenge for the pastor, pastoral assistant, or parish ministers—the "we" people in this chapter.

First Area of Challenge: Foster a Sense of Vocation. For many people, the job is something they do on the way to something else. We have to instill in them a sense of being called. But in doing this we have to be more inventive than we have been, for we instinctively return to churchy-clerical language to name this calling. We speak of the "priesthood" of the faithful and we speak of the "ministry" of the workplace. We call them a "priestly, prophetic, and kingly people." Such phrases are certainly valid, but they seem to imply altar and sanctuary connections. In short, such language seems to say that you are a holy layperson insofar as we can link you to traditional clerical categories with all the secular-sacred split that that might imply.

Fr. John Shea has a point in this regard. He reminds us that the church, like any big institution, tends to be self absorbed. So it creates needs and then recruits people to fill those needs. There is little concern over the independent work lives of the people. So, in the age of diminishing numbers of clergy, what is the agenda? Lay ministry! It's recruiting people for the internal structure of the church. That's surely a busy and necessary agenda, but it does tend to keep the official church from dealing fully with the vital question, the call to marketplace spirituality.

But we must keep the focus on the people's lives, and should not fudge their calling by speaking of the necessity of sanctuary ministers. Or, to put it another way, in any training of sanctuary ministers (anyone involved in official parish work or ministries), we must insist that their primary agenda is to facilitate others in the world. The lector, the eucharistic minister, the social concerns person, the cantor, the usher, the pastoral associate—all must not see themselves in terms of simply "getting people involved." They must see themselves in service to people where they are, to encourage them to recognize the presence of God, to discern God's action in their lives, to have a sensitivity to vocation, witness, and mission. Businessman John McDermott has this sensitivity when he says:

> This is our vocation, the vocation of the Catholic Christian layman and laywoman....It is a high calling. We are the Church in the world. We are the key social agents of the Church in the world. We are the religious insiders, inside secular society and its institutions. Without our knowledge, skill, power and commitment, the Church cannot fulfill its mission, cannot be Herself. Without us, without an awakened laity, the Church is in danger of becoming a weak and ineffective voice, confined to the sidelines and backwaters of American life.[1]

Another businessman says:

> I think of business as a vocation. It serves an obvious
> public function: it creates employment and it offers need-
> ed products and services to sustain and enhance
> life....Yet rarely have I heard business described as a vo-
> cation, either by clergy or by laity....The challenge we
> face is not only to do our work responsibly; it is also to
> find meaning in our work. Wouldn't the Christian con-
> cept of vocation help in this regard?[2]

I look at a popular Catholic magazine and see profiles of a
young Shakespearean actor, Leonardo Defilippis, doing inspir-
ing portrayals of the saints because he was searching for some
way that he could combine his theatrical abilities with a desire
to inspire others. Rolland Smith, a popular co-anchor of New
York Channel 9's prime time *News at Ten*, tries to display his
spirituality and convictions.[3] These are people who should *never* be pulled into sanctuary ministries, in the sense that such
ministries would be seen as superior to what they're doing and
where they're witnessing or where "real" service and spirituality can be found. We must instill in them and all the people we
deal with a profound sense of calling, a sense that they too,
wherever they are, are fair game for the Spirit. Remember, "ordinary people do not find their basic religious experiences inside churches but in the course of their daily lives. They go to
church to be reminded of the spiritual meaning of what they
experience outside of it all week long."[4]

But I want to carry these thoughts one step further. You notice that all these people speak of spirituality on the job. They
do have a sense of spirituality, of vocation. They continue to
say things like:

- I think of myself as empowering my colleagues, calling
  them from isolation—where they sought independence
  but found mostly constraint—to a common support for
  free *and* liberating work. I think it is religious work.

- As an academic layman, I am committed to two propositions: that there is one Truth; and that it matters.
- Each one of us is called to love and serve God, who loves us first.
- We frequently tend to compartmentalize our lives! Perhaps we must listen to the dismissal charge [at the end of Mass] and focus less on the "ended" and more on the exhortation to "love and serve the Lord." As Catholic Christians in the work world we must carry the gospel message into our workplaces and our communities.
- Sometimes I dream about a parish where the teaching and the preaching intentionally foster awareness of and pride in the Christian vocation.[5]

Add to these testimonies the new awareness of morality in everyday and in business life. I'm sure this is a reaction to the sorry public scandals—from Wall Street to the Pentagon—that have rocked the nation. Nevertheless, there is a decided "rebirth of ethics" in our country led by the universities.[6]

Still, of all of this you get a sense of an individual holiness, a sense of private effort. While we must praise this, I think we must note in all honesty that our collective impact remains small.[7] That is to say, while there has been more reflection and awareness and while there has been the enormous impact and popularity of Cursillo, Marriage Encounter, Focolare, and the various charismatic movements on individuals—and I admire all these programs and movements—it must be admitted that these movements are essentially inward looking. They have not added to but seem to have replaced the old activist Catholic guilds. Avery Dulles points out the demise of such groups as the Catholic Evidence Guild (literature and street corner preaching like Frank Sheed used to do in Hyde Park in London), the Young Christian Students Movement, the Catholic Interracial Guild, and many others. What became of them? Their disappearance has, in Dulles's words, resulted in

American culture not being sufficiently evangelized. In

spite of our many Catholic schools, colleges, and universities, we have as yet very few eminent Catholic intellec-
tuals on the national scene. Catholics, whether clerical or
lay, are not prominent in science, literature, the fine arts,
or even, I think, in the performing arts and communication. We have too few Catholic political leaders and
statesmen with a clear apostolic vision and commitment.

Perhaps as pastors or pastoral associates we might foster
"vocations" to these areas with the same sense of fulfillment
and zeal as we do for the ministerial priesthood and religious
life, and we might do what we can to restore those old guilds
and groups that were so formative in the lives of many. I guess
what I am saying is that any "sense of vocation" simply has to
move beyond the individual effort alone, beyond the "Jesus
and me" ratio, beyond simple awareness of the dignity of our
calling to a more penetrating awareness that "in unity there is
strength."

Still, for all this vision, it must be admitted that "being
Christian in the world" is difficult. What, for example, does it
mean to be a Christian? Is this an elitist notion or does it imply
a looking inward only? The Anti-Defamation League of B'nai
B'rith, for instance, criticizes liberation theology for being preoccupied with the concerns of the Third World and not at all
with Latin American Jews and Protestants. I think the difference is that the Christian acts on the principles of the gospel,
but always with the understanding that such principles are
shared with many other human beings. But perhaps, in practice, being a Christian in the world means some willingness *to
act differently and to be labeled as a serious believer.* In other
words, being a Christian in the world means tackling that most
pervasive pressure we have, namely, privatizing institutional
religion, making compartments out of our lives. That's the
practical crunch: acting differently without being a "religious
nut," to be known as a serious believer without the image of
the stern pilgrim or party pooper.

There are a few translations of this I would like to share:

1. Learning to love the world. This harks back to the "our world is evil" syndrome. But, after all, "God so loved the world that he gave his only Son, so that everyone who believes in him may not be lost but may have eternal life" (John 3:15). So our world is worth loving. That's worth remembering as we go off to work. Allied with this is:

2. Learning a sense of co-creation. This is offered as an antidote to finding a meaning to life as expressed through work. That's so critical. Meaning does not happen only after hours. It's there all the time and we must search for it. This in turn necessarily leads to:

3. Decisions in refusing to do any work one believes is not good. As Dolores Lecky points out:

> I know, for example, of television actors who have refused parts in a series because the roles denigrated the human person. I know of government workers who are seriously thinking about forgoing pensions and other benefits because of a growing crisis of conscience over the current United States military policy. And there are young couples who have deliberately chosen not to pursue the fast track to success but instead have chosen an alternate route, perhaps a lower rung on the economic ladder, in order to pursue creative work and to share in child care. Still others are choosing some form of volunteer ministry—for one year or two—spurred on by the search for meaning.[8]

I think immediately of former football star Bubba Smith turning down tons of money for making beer commercials (tough to do for a black athlete since they're not much in demand for commercials) after seeing the effects on adolescents. "As the years wear on, you stop compromising your principles" he said. Former Dallas Cowboys coach Tom Landry, an evangelical, says openly, "My position gives me an excellent platform from which to witness." These are basically those prophetic stances that take people's measure, but why not preach them, exhibit them, and make them a workable principle for market-place spirituality?

4. Common contemplation. Deliberately turning one's attention to the ordinary tasks of the moment—changing the tire, washing the windows, writing up an order, doing one's homework—can focus one's spirit, one's grasp for meaning.

5. Being aware of the people one works with. There are the boors, the dictators, the foul mouthed, the slackers, the dishonest, the incompatible—but all are one's "mission field." Silently picking out one to pray for that week helps give a sense of purpose and meaning as a Christian.

If you want another way of saying the same thing, Gerald Vandezande in a book entitled *Christians in the Crisis* gives wonderful guidelines for what he calls a "biblically faithful stewardship." Christians, he writes, must be *gentle* in the way they treat the environment; second, *just* in the way they treat their fellow workers; third, *wise* in the use of the creation's resources; fourth, *sensitive* to the needs of their neighbors as they pursue their tasks and vocations; fifth, *careful* in the way they use technology, so that they do not idolize technical know-how, but use it as a way of serving legitimate human goals; sixth, *frugal* in their patterns of energy consumption so that they do not waste the building blocks of the good life; seventh, *vigilant* in the prevention of waste; eighth, *fair* in the determination of prices; ninth, *honest* in the way they promote the sale of their products; and tenth, *equitable* in the earning of profit. Behind all these guidelines and suggestions are, once more, a need for support groups and associations that help keep the goal in focus.

❑ Lay Witness Sunday. For many years we've had one weekend dedicated to lay witness. On these occasions people get up at homily time (yes, I know they're not supposed to preach, but this is witnessing) to share how they try to translate faith in their lives and live by faith. We have singles, couples, and friends do it. We meet with them to clarify what their purpose is and then let them prepare. Frequently the married couples do a spoken duet with one alternating with the other in expressing their ideas. It's a powerful moment and well received.

6. Disciplining one's mental process for spirituality. Gregory Price expresses it:

I have no time for prayer and spirituality:
• I am extremely busy trying to make my new business a success.
• My wife and I had twins several months ago, and raising them takes up most of my free time.
• I feel a need to be involved in several community, political, and church organizations.

On the other hand, my prayer and spiritual life have never been better:
• I am extremely busy trying to make my new business a success.
• My wife and I had twins several months ago, and raising them takes up most of my free time.
• I feel a need to be involved in several community, political, and church organizations.

The answer to this paradox is the spirituality of work. This phrase is not mine. It was actually enunciated by Pope John Paul II in his recent encyclical, *On Human Work*....He means all of our daily activities—job, family and relationships, and community involvement—which help bring about the reign of God...work is simply all human activity that sustains and improves the world.

Spirituality can be defined as "the way we orient ourselves toward the divine." ...The basis for a spirituality of work is how one deals with the five major issues all people face at work: the meaning of their work, their relations with others, the integration of the various spheres of their lives, the ethics of what they are doing, and institutional maintenance and change.[9]

Under "integration of the spheres of life" Pierce quotes John Shea in saying that the challenge here is to balance four areas: responsibilities to our job and families; workaholism; burnout caused by not integrating work and play; and integrity.

If you want a couple of neat charts that catch the whole idea of marketplace spirituality and responsibility, there are two on pages 26-27 that are worth looking at.

Second Area of Challenge: Facilitate the Conversation with Tradition. To appreciate this category we must breeze through a little history. The New Testament reveals a people impacted by Jesus and by their own quest to discover how to live their newfound faith in the world, in their context. The Fathers of the church and the early monks also had as their object the quest of spiritual wisdom and union with God. But this quest, of course, had to be shared ("Go, teach all nations"), and in spreading the gospel the apostles and their followers necessarily had to come to terms with a Greek world of philosophy and metaphysics. People like Clement of Alexandria (d. 215) and Origen (d. 252) met the challenge by pioneering the Good News into the systematic science of theology, but still a theology whose main thrust was seeking the way to spiritual wisdom, a lived theology.

But the heresies of the fourth and fifth centuries added their impact and forced an even more careful and scientific framing of theology. This required the talents of such experts as Athanasius, Cyril of Alexandria, St. Augustine, and all the rest of the great ecumenical councils figures. Surely all this reactionary and necessary precision was a great boon, but it did have its negative side: theology came to be seen precisely as the property of experts and consequently beyond the competence of the ordinary people. This was further enforced in the Middle Ages with the rise of cathedral schools in Charlemagne's time (ninth century), the great universities of the twelfth century, and, most of all, with the rediscovery of the Greek philosophers and their rational ways of thinking. That's why, in time, the university and not the church became the place for "doing" theology, and why theology was done by the "head" people,

Master Image Chart

Image	Goal in the Business World	Most Developed Character Traits	Least Developed Character Traits
Millionaire	To accumulate capital and live in luxury	Persistence and ingenuity	Sensitivity to the needs of others and justice
King of the Mountain	To wield powers over others	Toughness and cleverness	Compassion
Craftsperson	To see the job well done	Fidelity to standards	Flexibility
Company person	To help people develop and to protect company interests	Loyalty	Independence from company and creativity
Gamesman	To be a winner at whatever one does to solve problems	Coolness under stress and ability	Intimacy and generosity
Captain on the bridge	To maintain control by appeasing interest groups	Flexibility	Idealism

Judeo-Christian Values	Contrasting Values
1. Value of power over individuals in service to help others develop their unique gifts (Phil. 2:1:18; John 13: 1-14).	Value of power over individuals as domination and control of others.
2. Value of power over nature as a stewardship by persons over *God's* world. Persons are called to transform nature in harmony with the whole of creation (Genesis 1:26-31).	Value of power over nature as a mandate to produce a maximum of consumer goods and creature comforts.
3. Value of wealth and property as an opportunity for increased service for mankind, yet as a *possible* obstacle to salvation (Luke 16:19-31).	Value of wealth and property as the measure of a person's worth.
4. Value of happiness as achieved through God's intentions for humankind (Mark 8:36).	Value of happiness as achieved through acquiring possessions.
5. Value of justice as the right of each person's means of leading a human life (Acts 2:42-17).	Value of justice as the protection of property already possessed.
6. Value of deferring gratification of wants (John 12:22-26; Luke 14:27).	Value of immediate gratification of wants
7. Value of time as reverence for God (Luke 12:22-32).	Value of time as money.

Any sense of vocation can be guided by the questions these charts raise.

the academicians. And the purpose of doing theology was no longer primarily to attain spiritual wisdom to live by, but to develop clarity and rational knowledge about God to think by. In short, theology, called "the queen of sciences," became severed from the spirituality of everyday life. Talking first *to* God was no longer required in order to talk *about* God.

With the sixteenth-century Protestant Reformation the church had to respond defensively, with the theologians leading the counterattack. From this counterattack emerged a new style of theology called "dogmatic theology." This was a system that started out with a given thesis (the church's official position) and then worked backwards to prove the thesis. In other words, theologians would cite a dogmatic thesis of the church and then "prove" it by appealing to the church's book of collected dogmas (commonly called "Denzinger," after its compiler), a simple numbered compilation with no historical context. This circular system was what Avery Dulles called "regressive theology," that is, going backwards to "find" the answers you've already given.

This sort of thesis theology, cemented in place by the attacks of the eighteenth-century Enlightenment and the twentieth-century Modernist heresy, lasted from about 1690 to 1950 and was a theology that, unlike Thomas Aquinas's, started off with the answer (he started off with the question) and worked to prove it. The results, of course, were packaged into catechisms and passed on to the people in a kind of "trickle-down theology." The whole venture was a theology done by experts out of touch with the real world. For that matter, it was a theology of only a small part of the world, the Latin, western European part. It was a theology that lived in isolation from the vast movements of the artistic, educational, and scientific communities. Most of all, it was an isolated, vertical, "imposed" theology separated from the real lives of real people.

Anyway, what's the point of this survey? The point is that we are now in an era when the trickle-down thesis theology of the experts is giving way to dialoguing with the "percolating-up theology" of the People of God. We are living in an era when once more we are invited to participate in and contribute to the theological enterprise. It's like the principle behind liberation, black, and feminist theologies: listen to the experience of the people! That, too, is a rich source of wisdom. Let that also be a factor in theologizing and let such experience be the link between theology and spirituality. If the call is to universal holiness, then look at the gospel from the ground up. Consider: How does the peasant in the Brazilian barrio understand God's word? How does he identify with a Lazarus at the door where we do not? How does a feminist respond to the story of the woman at the well? Does he or she see it as a story of inclusion, acceptance, equality, and discipleship? Do blacks see the Good Samaritan story with fresh eyes? Is it not possible that God's self-disclosure arises from contemporary experience *as well as* from the ancient texts? And shouldn't they interrelate?

In short, as Tom Groome says, "Theology done from and by the people will undoubtedly need to be enlightened and enriched by the work of experts, but the theological enterprise must not be left to those experts alone. In fact, the experts must be in dialogue with and reflecting upon the faith life of people as much as the people need to take account of the research of the scholars."[10] So our task is not to teach the people *what* to think but *how* to think about their Christian lives in the world. We go to the people not just to discover a new technique for reaching them, but in order to be with them and to encourage them to name their experience.

So, once again, our task as pastoral ministers is to mediate the Tradition with the people and in turn help the people to ask the Tradition, "Do you have anything to say to me? Anything to help me?" To put it another way, we must help contemporary experience prosecute the Tradition and help the Tradition critique the contemporary experience. We must facilitate the dialogue between trickle-down and percolate-up, between our people's experience and the ancient Tradition. We must open their voices to contribute to theology and to reconnect theology to everyday spirituality.

Of course, all this implies two serious mandates for the pastoral minister. First, he or she must know the Tradition—so earnest study (via courses, seminars, workshops, sabbaticals) is a moral obligation. Second, he or she must also know the people. This is an important part of the new agenda for the future parish and we play a most critical part in this agenda.

Third Area of Challenge: Promote Storytelling Groups. More prosaically, we must promote support groups of every kind. Such groups supply the raw material for the dialogue with the Tradition. People should be encouraged to meet and, in the light of the Tradition and Scripture, recount their stories and try to discover what's going on in their lives. Furthermore, they need support groups to help them discover strategies and find encouragement for marketplace witness and spirituality. In short, the storytelling or support groups help members to think about daily work experiences from a Christian perspective. Here's some sharings from such groups:

Just this afternoon, I walked into a courtroom as a lawyer for the first time and gathered in yet another harvest to owners I have never seen.

I lost my job. After thirty years. The roof caved in. It was the worst thing that ever happened. My family, my faith got me through it.

So, if there's a labor meeting, I show up. It's my vocation to be there.

A group of us began to get together on Saturday mornings to talk about where God had been in our lives that week. These were high-powered people. They began to open up, to trust one another. I got help on concrete problems. It was the best church I ever had.

There used to be two choices for Catholic women—get married or become a nun. There's got to be another way. I'm a successful business woman, single, and on my own. The Lord put me in touch with other loving people who need me and who let me need them.[11]

There are as many shared stories as there are such groups. Moreover, in the context of such groups often daring new insights can be gained that tap the "subversive memory" of the Tradition (something back there pops up to challenge us here). Here, for example, is a story shared by one woman after reading Canadian author Gabrielle Roy's book, *The Road to Alamont*. She read to the group the part where a little girl named Christine is sent to the Canadian wilds to live with Grandma— and is bored to death. She only comes somewhat alive when Grandma offers to make her a doll:

> Incredulous that dolls could be found anywhere but in stores, she goes nevertheless to the attic and brings down her grandmother's big scrap bag. With bits of cloth and oats as stuffing, yellow yarn for hair, and a piece of curtain lace and blue ribbon which fashioned the dress, the grandmother creates a beautiful doll with a painted face and real leather shoes. Awed by the creativity of the old woman, a sense of grandeur, of infinite solitude came over the little girl. "You're like God," she wept into her ear. "You're just like God. You can make things out of nothing as he does."

Later on, Christine has a dream and this is how she describes it:

> In my dream God the Father, with his great beard and stern expression, yielded his place to Grandmother, with her keen, far-seeing eyes. From now on it would be she, seated in the clouds, who would take care of the world, set up wise and just laws. Now all would be well for the poor people on earth....For a long time I was haunted by the idea that it could not possibly be a man who made the world, but perhaps an old woman with extremely capable hands.[12]

In this, of course, both the author and the woman recounting the story are stretching the notion of God in the best biblical tradition where, for example, in Psalm 18 God is called rock, fortress, deliverer, shield, horn of my salvation; or an eagle, a mother hen, shepherd, door, way and so on. Again, it is in just such sharing groups that such insights are possible.

Finally, since there is usually a wide diversity in the average parish, diversity in age, work, lifestyles, interests, etc., it is to the parish's advantage to see itself as a "community of communities," offering the unity of a common worship and place and the diversity of expressions of the same gospel. Once more, the pastoral minister should encourage storytelling groups wherever such groups find it advantageous to meet.[13]

In the next chapter we will continue what might be a new agenda for pastors and pastoral ministers when we take up the fourth and fifth challenges.

CHAPTER 3

New Agenda
Part 2

Fourth Area of Challenge: Help Catholics to Be catholic.
The small "c" of the last word catches something of what I
want to say here in purely practical terms. Consider the common crisis of many dioceses in our country (and of course in
many others): there is a severe shortage of priests (felt more in
some areas than others, but nevertheless real across the board).
Local population changes have emptied some parishes. Whole
new parish configurations and staffing patterns are in order.
Some parishes must consolidate and others be closed. Indeed,
that is already happening. There has been proposed (with
much uproar) that 48 parishes in Detroit be shut down. Bishop
Wuerl of Pittsburgh issued a pastoral letter at the end of 1988
reporting that from 1976 to 1986 parishes lost almost 113,000

registered Catholics. Forty-two parishes and missions have lost over 45 percent of their population. In other areas, parishes are growing more than expected.

In Albany, Bishop Hubbard said pretty much the same thing. He cited a net decline of 58 active priests in 10 years, leaving 262 priests to serve 200 parishes. As everywhere, many urban parishes are overstaffed (as a hangover from past glories) and many suburban parishes are understaffed, with only one priest for 1000 to 2000 families. Many dioceses are appointing task forces to try to discover strategies to keep some parishes open, close others, consolidate still others, and yet preserve the commitment to Catholic schools and promote vocations to the priesthood, vocations that are so low as to threaten the future supply (unless, of course, there is a more liberal allowance for the criteria for ordination) and to prepare for more shared and collaborative ministries.

In this present crisis, clearly the task for the pastoral minister (and other leaders and hierarchy) is to make Catholics more catholic; that is, (1) help them see themselves as church and (2)—and I want to give this special emphasis since it's a very practical matter—to educate them to the wider needs of the Catholic community. We have done this more or less well for the foreign missions and outreach programs, but not at all for our own sense of mutuality. The whole parish structure in fact militates against any larger concerns. The priest is involved in his parish, as are the parishioners. There are no or few mechanisms to interact and feel responsible regionally. Local finances, duplicated programs, schools, activities, and that invisible but operating attitude that this is "my" plant are the order of the day. Competition, friendly or otherwise, is taken for granted. In short, neither parish clergy nor people (nor bishop for that matter) emotionally think beyond their parish enclave or feel a responsibility for the church as a whole in a particular diocese. (My theory is that dioceses themselves are too large and place an impossible burden on the bishop to build cohesion or community). When parishes are proposed to be closed or consolidated, the cry reaches to heaven because no one is pre-

pared for the wider needs nor trained to the wider vision of local church.

Some twenty-five years ago I had a thought that I shared
with my bishop at the time, a thought he rejected but which I
think is still valid today—and perhaps even more so. I'm sure
there are some civil and canonical or legal difficulties to overcome, but basically here is what I proposed. First, the situation:
At that time there was a vast population movement in our diocese, with a huge Levittown (since renamed) of several thousand homes being built. The usual diocesan strategy was to
buy property and build a church and a school. Period. I was
alarmed for the following reasons: (1) No single church would
ever be large enough to handle the crowds anticipated in the
mammoth development; (2) more severely, by putting in a
large parish and school, the diocese was strapping the parish
with a 30-year mortgage that would ensure that it would never, could never, be split during that time because a large financial base would be needed to pay off the debt and support the
ongoing needs; the result (3) was that the parish would soon
be too small for the needs of such a large community. We
would end up with another one of those megatron parishes
that are beyond the ability of the clergy to serve in any way beyond "keeping the plant going"; certainly, at least, we would
force the pastor into full-time administration. And with such a
large, impersonal parish, when the 1970s and 1980s came with
their upsurge of fundamentalist preachers and poachers, Catholics looking for smaller communities and certainties and plain
recognition would be fair game.

❑ My proposal to the bishop was this (again, legalities to be
considered): Instead of erecting a specific parish in a crowded
(or soon to be crowded) area, announce that you are planting
"The Catholic Presence" or, if you will, "A Catholic Federation" in the area. So a parish church is built, but the people
(who are in on the planning from the start) understand *from the
beginning* that this church is but a part of a larger witnessing
Catholic presence which, in time, will spawn other parish
churches to form ultimately, let's say, the Catholic Federation

of Jonesville. To underscore this where it matters (besides a great deal of public relations from the chancery and the bishop), the collection envelope would be designed from the beginning with the information that 5 or 10 percent (or whatever) would be put in escrow to be used to give birth to another expression of the Catholic presence in the region (whether it is a parish church or a school or a retreat house or whatever).

Furthermore, from the beginning, a task force from that parish should be designated to monitor the needs of the church in the region and give advice on where the next expansion might take place—and such a task force should have an automatic place on the parish council. When the time comes to build another parish, a great fuss and ceremony should accompany the birthing of an offspring parish with, of course, the handing over of the escrow seeding money.

What I'm after is a wider attitude, a larger vision of church in this or that area. From the beginning, the theme of movement and expansion should be kept in the forefront; and although we all desire a stable parish home, we can still stretch our vision to help others build theirs. If, from the start, part of our money has gone into that vision and our missionary sense has been nurtured, if the anticipated "birthing" rituals and mechanisms are in place, it might be easier to overcome the once-and-for-all planted parish that is turned inward, frozen in its spot, and resentful of the intrusions and needs of others, even in the very same diocese.

I realize that this is much more the problem of the higher-ups, the diocesan shakers and movers, but still, the local pastoral minister can try to share a vision of church and help Catholics to be a bit more catholic.

And perhaps we should try not only to help the people to be more catholic in their horizontal expansiveness, but also in their vertical expansiveness. By that I mean that sometimes we operate (mostly unconsciously, I think) like a dysfunctional family by promoting the addiction of an immature co-dependency. The laity have low spiritual self-esteem and the clergy are the spiritual "experts" (first prejudice again) with the result that the lay-clerical relationship often falls into a parent-child relationship—something (and here's the dysfunction) that is both allowed and *desired* on both sides. The clergy want to act like a parent; the laity want to act like a child. And so there's the problem and the challenge. The problem is that there will be no marketplace spirituality without the clergy's "permission" or approval. The challenge is to establish an adult mentality in the clergy-laity relationship, to build up the spiritual self-esteem of the laity. Leo the Great's dictum must be theirs: "Christian, know your dignity!" The notion of co-discipleship (Archbishop May), the releasing of the power within the believing community, are all agendas. And, in a very practical and gentle way, to let the people know that they have in Canon Law not only rights but legal procedures.

To be Catholic is to be universal, expansive up and down, within and without.

Fifth Area of Challenge: Provide Now for Spiritual Direction and Discipline in preparation for the New Asceticism. Now that the third prejudice is breaking down—that spiritual direction was the preserve of the clergy and religious—and now that people desire to both name and discern their religious experiences and foster their vocations, we must provide the opportunity for spiritual direction and guidance in the spiritual exercises. (Later on I'll speak of a parish spiritual director). Training in formal prayer, the encouragement and resources for Scripture study groups, guided spiritual reading, devotions, etc., are all needed opportunities. Most of all the pastoral minister, by giving priority to the spiritual life, can give that affirmation and legitimization (permission if you will) that people need so much in order to walk with the Lord openly and freely both at home and in the marketplace.

I say that this is all in preparation for the new asceticism because I note the following trends. First, there is an evident rebirth of faith gestating in reaction to the excesses of the 1960s and 1970s. One potent example: an article in *The New York Times* (December 29, 1988) by John Wheeler, who is the president of the Center for the Vietnam Generation, points out that "questions of faith and spirit" are evident wherever he goes among his fellow Baby Boomers—the more than 60 million of them—who have now entered midlife. Wheeler points out that a survey found that 69 percent of them believe in God or a positive spiritual force, and 49 percent "reported they had become more spiritual in the last five years." Why, he asks? He lists three reasons.

1. The United States is in a "season of remembrance," which means that we are returning to our roots. This is evident in the extraordinary amount of memorials being built around the country: the Vietnam Wall in Washington D.C., memorials for black patriots, the Korean War, women in military service, the Holocaust, etc. Right now Americans are building 143 major Vietnam memorials. What does all this mean? "Memorials awaken questions of faith" he says. "Are there things worth dying for? Is death the last word?"

2. The theme of midlife passage (which those 60 million plus are going through right now) is affirmation of fundamental values. "For many, the re-evaluation and affirmation of faith happen because life awakens us to the spiritual void caused by fixation on money and material possessions, by marital infidelity and by self-concern (our oldest nemesis, pride)."

3. Science itself is the third reason for the return to spirituality. In their exploration of the universe, scientists are running into such mystery that they can no longer use the old scientific language. It is inadequate. They are turning to the language of the medieval mystics.

All this dovetails with the January 1989 Gallup poll that shows that, for 86 percent of American adults, religion is very to fairly important in their lives. There does seem to be a religious renaissance abroad and we have to meet the challenge—and have confidence in the "product" we are offering in response to faith's need. Furthermore, along with the challenge to a people who are seeking a mature faith, there is, as Wheeler implied above, the correlative need for spiritual discipline that has made people open to what I call the new asceticism. And this desire for the new asceticism is not the just wishful thinking of a professional cleric, but rather a realistic assessment by many people confronted by two current and inescapably harsh realities.

The first [reality] is the physical environment. Newspaper headlines tell us that "To Beat the Greenhouse Effect Lives Must Be Changed": [Experts say] we can live in airtight houses, work under energy-stingy florescent lights, keep our food in refrigerators cooled with new, safe chemicals, drive cars that get 70 miles to the gallon, warm homes with natural gas or solar heat. To be sure, none of this comes without cost. Or we can go on living our lives as usual...and wind up in a world that changes drastically.

James Gustave Speth, President of World Resources Institute says:

People everywhere are offended by pollution. They sense intuitively that we have pressed beyond limits we should not have exceeded. They want to clean up the world, make it a better place, be good trustees of the earth for future generations.

People, at least in the United States, have to come to terms, for example, with the car—a very tender spot since the automobile mystique is in our very bones. But think—our country has 180 million of them! The next nearest country, Brazil, has 11 million. (China has 761,000). We never think that the metals used to make cars are nonrenewable resources extracted from ore that damages the environment with pollutants from the mining sites. Then there's the costs of petroleum extraction, destruction from building roads, bridges, parking garages, shopping centers, gas stations, and of course, the exhaust that contributes to lung cancer, emphysema, acid rain, and the greenhouse effect.[2] (We haven't mentioned that more deaths occur from car accidents every single year than the sum total

of deaths in the Vietnam War). As the Soviet cosmonaut, Alex-
ei Yeliseev, who has spent more than 210 hours in space, notes:

> It's not only that you look down on the planet and see
> there are no boundaries. Rather, it is that you see for
> yourself, with your own eyes, how small the globe is.
> And you see the pollution. When a polluted river gets to
> the ocean, you see a huge smear. And you see smoke—
> from cities, from forests being burned off. You see all
> sorts of pollutants—and you see no place other than earth
> where we can live.

It's no surprise, therefore, that for the first time in its history, *Time* magazine did not have for 1988 a Man or Woman of
the Year but rather the "Planet of the Year." Its promotional
blurb reads:

> What on earth are we doing?
> No single individual or event dominated the
> news in 1988 more than this fragile clump of
> rock, soil, air and water we call home.
> This week's *Time* names endangered earth
> Planet of the Year—and presents a worldwide
> agenda to save the planet.
> The poisoning of our planet: to this issue that
> transcends boundaries, *Time* brings a voice of
> global reach and influence—and the attention
> of the world's leaders.

Well, beyond the desire to sell the magazine, the point
should be obvious. We need discipline, an asceticism to come
to terms with all this and people must have—indeed desire to
have—motivation for both. Still, I would suggest that our emphasis be not on doomsdaying but on beauty: seeing, appre-
ciating, preserving it, and recognizing its power.

The second reality is the spiritual or relational environment
that is just as badly abused and scarred. The enshrined agenda

of the past decades was that anything that smacked of external discipline, external constraint (dubbed "medieval"—which in turn meant church interference) or that might cause guilt or undue "repression" must be systematically done away with. After all, decency, fair play, and justice would come "from within." People were enlightened enough to make enlightened moral decisions by themselves. (Pelagianism lives.) Well, the horrors of the Holocaust, the "killing fields" of Cambodia and the Ukraine, the epidemic of drugs that still saps our national strength, insider trading deals, child abuse, abortions, violence, teenage pregnancies, and broken marriages, the litany of such things that we live with daily all give the lie to that agenda. Or, in a snappier vein, as the inimitable Tom Wolff describes it:

The great American Contribution to the 20th century's start from zero was in the area of manners and mores, especially in what was rather primly called "the sexual revolution." In every hamlet, even in the erstwhile Bible Belt, may be found the village brothel, no longer hidden in a house of blue lights or red lights behind a green door but openly advertised by the side of the road with a thousand-watt black-lit plastic sign: "Totally All-Nude Girl Sauna Massage And Marathon Encounter Sessions Inside."

Until several years ago, pornographic movie theaters were as ubiquitous as the 7-Eleven: these theaters included outdoor drive-ins with screens six, seven, eight stories high, the better to beam all the moistened folds and glistening nodes and stiffened giblets to a panting American countryside. But since then, in the last two years or so, the pornographic movies have begun to be replaced by the pornographic videocassette, which could be brought into any home.

Up on the shelf in the den, next to the set of *The Encyclopedia Brittanica* and the great books, one now finds the cassettes: "Shanks Akimbo," "That Thing with the Cup."

My favorite moment in Jessica Hahn's triumphal tour of Medialand this fall came when a 10-year-old girl, a student at a private school, wearing a buttercup blouse, a cardigan sweater and her school uniform skirt, approached her outside a television studio with a stack of Playboy magazines featuring the famous Hahn nude form and asked her to autograph them. With the school's blessing, she intended to take the signed copies back to the campus and hold a public auction. The proceeds would go to the poor.

But in the sexual revolution, too, the painful dawn has already arrived, and the relearning is imminent. All may be summed up in a single term, requiring no amplification: AIDS.[3]

People sense, then, that our society is sick. One more example: In an essay on public television, Roger Rosenblatt said, "When asked by Representative Les Aspin what it was that prompted the recent Pentagon thievery, the third-ranking Pentagon official, Robert B. Costello, answered, "Greed." The Wall Street thieves are driven by greed. So were the TV evangelists, the Bakkers, the arms merchants in the Iran/Contra scandal. Rosenblatt calls greed "the word of the year" and reminds us that one can be greedy for things other than money: "for power, for fame, for experience, for influence, even for affection." He adds, "The basis of the sin is excess. Take any normal healthy impulse, misshape it into freakish lust, ignore the demands of moderation and there you have it."

This drive to excess is very much fired by advertising. As one of its representatives says, in an interview in the *Wall Street Journal*, "All of us in advertising are pushing consumption. If you don't buy, we're all in trouble." Until the Wall Street crash in 1987 the main target was the yuppies, and the most telling ad was the one for Michelob Light "Who says you can't have it all?" David Carlin, a politician who writes for *Commonweal*, has this to say:

After a binge of secularism that now has extended twenty-five years, we find ourselves living with drugs, AIDS, poverty, homelessness, divorce, abortion, out-of-wedlock births, functional illiteracy, cultural illiteracy, etc., while vast numbers of the "more fortunate" are engaged in the indecent exercise of getting and spending as much as they can.

Rosenblatt piggybacks this observation:

When our self-interest becomes uninterest in others, when personal acquisition becomes another person's loss in the social network, when my too much means your too little, that is how one knows [there is imbalance]. Intriguingly, this humanist social observer warns that desire is infinite. It does not stop and only God can handle infinity. Maybe that's why greed is called a sin.[4]

There's a lot of the gospel in these remarks from secular sources and this emphasizes once more that "the time is ripe" for the new asceticism. At this time in history, with our physical and spiritual environments crying out for redemption, spiritual direction, retreats, and discipline have a critical part to play in the healing process. They are not niceties for the spiritually elite. They are necessities for the humanly alert.

There is a confirming word to this judgment from a practiced observer of the American spiritual landscape. Art Winter is the editor of *Praying*, a bimonthly published by the *National Catholic Reporter*. In a recent issue (January-February 1989) he took a poll of the national retreat scene and noted seven major trends in the retreat movement.

1. From morality to spirituality. That is, the emphasis is no longer on just "me and my sin," but on learning how to pray so that you can have a personal relationship with Jesus. Christ is the (new) center, not morality as in the retreat days of old when one examined one's conscience and worked toward the retreat's high point: confession.

2. Toward a holistic spirituality. There is not just the vertical

preoccupation between God and the soul, but rather a concern about total health: physical, mental, psychological, and spiritual.

3. Interest in contemplative prayer. This used to be associated with religious communities but now is popular among lay people, especially those turning to Thomas Merton and his method of "centering prayer" popularized by Father Basil Pennington.

4. Rise in healing ministry. There are so many hurts and more and more retreats are based on the Twelve Step Program of Alcoholics Anonymous.

5. This worldly emphasis in spirituality. The emphasis here is not just on the individual but on all creation, a kind of environmental spirituality we hinted at above. This in turn forms a basis for social justice. Interestingly, we find another confirmation from the country's retreat masters. Although a kind of environmental or creation-centered spirituality is growing in popularity and is a basis for social justice concerns, nevertheless, the report is that such concerns remain weak. The retreat masters remind us that it wasn't always so. Up through the 1930s retreatants used to study the social encyclicals and how to implement them. This approach faded well before Vatican II and only now is making a small comeback. As one retreat master observed, "Social justice remains a hard sell because many people want to hear about God and their relationship with God, but only a few seem willing to take the next step—that this relationship is linked to their neighbor."

6. From one to many. Now there are many formats, from small group process to sharing.

7. Increased role of lay people. In America, by and large, it has been the lay people who have made the retreats, and they have done so far more than the religious who gave the retreats. Now, in a dramatic extension, the laity are also on the organizational end of retreats. That is, they are on the retreat house staffs, are often the directors of retreat houses, and give spiritual direction and conferences. Women are especially prominent here.

Art Winter's survey seems to verify the contours of what we have been saying. It's a survey that the pastoral minister can use in making up the New Agenda.

Finally, in this context I'd like to mention what I think is an unexplored area in spirituality that is crying to be noticed and developed. That area is friendship. This is an acute question for singles. In the United States, 41 percent of the population are young adults between the ages of 18 and 34 (about half of whom, by the way, have dropped out of church). This is roughly about fifteen million young Catholic adults. But the thing to remember is that our current culture usually allows only two stances for such people (or for teens): in relationships one is either a stranger or a lover (genital sex). We have allowed friendship as a way of life and of spirit to fall by the wayside. But now with the dreaded AIDS there's a new opportunity to explore the area of friendship. And people are ready to hear this message. I recall being taken aback by the eager response at a conference of Young Adults when in a general talk I merely alluded to the whole area of friendship. They dearly wanted to know more about it. And this includes the area of spiritual friendship:

> A male and female friendship is thus a place of creative tension in which the encounter with the other—a disquieting experience in itself—is heightened by the experience of being drawn so completely out of the self by desire. But, by maintaining its own specific life as friendship and by not becoming either a union of lovers or marriage or by not retreating into the cool and safely negotiated corridors of acquaintance, men and women's spiritual friendships come to embody some of the dynamics and gifts of both marriage and celibacy.[5]

Nor should we forget men in this whole question of friendship. According to Elliot Engel of North Carolina State, the male twosome is designed more for combat than for comfort. Men are expected to compete and their growing up message is "Show any weakness and we'll clobber you with it." Getting

ahead and dominating, doing, producing, having—all super-
sede wives, children, and friendships. The women? They are
different. This same Elliot Engel tells of the time his family was
moving away and how his wife's best friend came in for a final
goodbye:

> Their last hugs were so painful to witness that I finally
> had to turn away and leave the room. I've always been
> amazed at the nurturing, emotional support my wife can
> seek and return with her close female friends. Her three-
> hour talks with friends refresh her and renew her far
> more than my three-mile jogs restore me. In our society it
> seems as if you've got to have a bosom to be a buddy.[6]

Leading psychologists and therapists estimate that only
about 10 percent of men have real friendships. This whole lack
of an effective life and expression takes its toll:

> The death rate for males is 200 percent higher in the early
> 20s than for females. From 30 on it is twice as high....Men
> are four times more likely to die from bronchitis, emphy-
> sema, and asthma than women....Men also have much
> higher death rates from hypertension, from pneumonia
> and influenza, and from cancer. Men do not cope well
> with severe emotional problems either.[7]

It's hard to resist mentioning here a report issued to priests
November 1988, and to the public in December 1988, from the
Bishops' Committee on Priestly Life and Ministry. That report
said that many of the 53,000 priests in the country are over-
worked, lonely, and sexually troubled. The priest's sexuality,
therefore, should be recognized as an "essential component of
human existence" and, as a consequence, better methods, including the encouragement of close friendships with men and
women, need to be found to help priests live a celibate life. So
it would seem that the investigation of the unexplored area of
friendship is valid not only for the public in general and men

in particular, but also for those men who are our priests. In any case, sensitive pastoral ministers will try to respond to this new need for friendship and include this as part of spiritual direction as well as in the other four areas we mentioned. These, after all—sense of vocation, conversation with tradition, storytelling groups, helping Catholics be catholic, and providing spiritual direction—are the New Agenda for a new century.

CHAPTER 4

Pastoral
Reflections

This and the other reflection chapter at the end of the book are the kind you can skip. They're a little more probing and exploratory, which is a way of saying that I'm thinking out loud because I don't have the answers—and perhaps not even the proper questions. Anyway, I want to explore further some of the "new agenda" thoughts from the previous chapters, especially those concerned with the everyday spirituality and mission of the people.

My first reflection centers around a notable and glaring fact: Catholics have "arrived!" Not only are they in the mainstream, they are at the *top* of the mainstream. Catholics represent, for example, 30 percent of *Fortune* magazine's 500 most successful business people, are well represented in the high command of the military, business, and Congress. Already Catholic laity constitute 80 percent of the personnel in parochial education and are moving quickly to 90 percent. They are in huge numbers in ministry and health careers.

The people at the big Harvard futurist think tank maintain that there are really only four truly global institutions: the United Nations, the Multinational corporations, International Terrorists—and the Catholic Church. In short, this time in history could be, given our numbers and positions, what Pastor Richard Neuhaus calls "The Catholic Moment." Yet, it is not. For all the facts and figures there is no discernible Catholic "presence" in this country. Why, I wonder? Some responses surely must include secularization, but beyond that it seems the deeper problem is privatization. Catholic piety and belief are disconnected from everyday life. Catholic piety, belief, and awareness are disconnected from the rest of the globe.

As to the latter, the average American Catholic (like Americans in general) are geographically and politically chauvinistic. There is a big church out there, far more numerous and growing than the model we're used to. Our model (and experience) is a European and Irish one (rapidly shrinking). But there's a growing global church that includes Africa, South America, Asia, and elsewhere. Even in this country you see more and more Hispanic and Asian faces in church. You know times are changing when, in a story from Joe Holland, an American native of Asian heritage called for information and was told to contact a Mr. Doyle. And she asked how to spell Doyle! Our sense of mission just doesn't seem to have a global awareness and reach out to it. At least knowing we have this lack is a challenge for any pastoral minister. Ponder Avery Dulles's words:

> The dimension of catholicity most prominent in modern theological discussion is the quantitative or geographical. The church is broadly inclusive because it is spread across the face of the globe. ...Catholicity in this sense is opposed to every kind of sectarianism or religious indi-

vidualism....The church is a communion of variously gifted individuals and communities, bound together by relationships of mutual openness and complementarity. The
church's capacity, with its profound inner unity, to break
down the barriers between different peoples is repeatedly
celebrated in the NT and early Christian literature....

Each major period of church history has a special task
or vocation of its own. The apostolic age laid the founda-
tions once and for all, but left many things unfinished.
The patristic period established the basic structures of the
church's ministry, dogma and sacramental life. The Middle Ages worked out with great subtlety and complete-
ness the applications of the Christian faith to a given culture, i.e. medieval Europe. The modern period, taking up
a broader missionary task, carried Christianity to all con-
tinents. Our own age, it would seem, has the assignment
to incarnate the gospel in the cultures of diverse peoples
of non-European stock.[1]

That "assignment" would seem to be a first step in making
effective "the Catholic Moment."

As for being disconnected from everyday life, it's Pope John
Paul II himself who not only sees the problem but has given us
a threefold division to consider: vocation, communion, and
mission. As to vocation, we are reminded that we should no
longer define ourselves in the negative, for example, by saying
that the laity are *not* bishops, *not* priests, etc. We must remember that Vatican II's dogmatic Constitution on the Church began with the inner life of the church and placed its section on
the People of God as a whole and its section on the laity *before*
the section on the hierarchy. So the People of God have a vocation. There is a call through baptism—a call that is personal
while also being a call to communion. This communion (the
pope's second point) is the communion or unity of all in the
church—that the Christian enterprise is a shared and collaborative reality. To this degree, the call is to unity first before we
ever approach the world. To this degree, we leaders must keep

before the people and promote reconciliation—between priests and bishops, clergy and laity, etc.—before mission can be viable. It's a spiritual, healing agenda we're talking about.

But there are problems, as we know, in this notion of unity or communion and reconciliation, and we must reflect on them, too. Ministry itself is divisive because it is still a hard word to define and pin down. Ministry's structures are diverse. They run from Honduras's or the South Pacific's thousands of catechists to Brazil's or Zaire's base communities. Then you have to mix in the vexing question of associations and movements like the Focolare, charismatics, Marriage Encounter, cursillo, Opus Dei, and other worldwide ecclesial movements. What is their relationship to the local and universal church?

What about ordained ministry and the place of women? We have to deal with these questions before we can discover the unity that enables us to move effectively into mission, for mission is a natural consequence of communion. If one is called to communion with Christ and with others, then the natural outcome is to ask: called for what purpose? Mission is the flip side of the call. Union always demands mission. If you love someone you naturally must *do* something. In Carlo Carretto's version of St. Francis's conversion experience he has him say:

Yes, now I saw the sun, the moon, the earth, the springs, the flowers...but now they spoke to me....Everything seems new to me. I began to grasp that God was all around me, and had sent those marvelous messengers, creatures, before his face. I felt that he wished to speak to me. So I kept repeating, "What do you want me to do, Lord?"

So to be in communion is by nature to be sent. True, but once more, we are victims of an intense privatization caused no doubt by our longstanding inferior status in America, American high individualism, and the impact of a highly secular and absolutist "separation" of the church and state that socially and legally seeks to keep religion a matter of private taste. So, even if called, even if united, even if sent, we hesitate to go. We don't want to intrude. What people do is their business. We don't want to "impose" our values on others (in spite of a massive consumer media that does just that).

In spite of all these obstacles, what's all this vocation-communion-mission mean in practice? The answer to this seems to come back to an old point: it means for one thing that we cannot give the impression that the priest's job is to build up the Christian community and the laity's job is in the world, as if there were two separate realms. It means that we the leaders have to stop talking in dual terms:

> What bedevils our pastoral theology and daily practice is the "churchy" mindset that automatically expects Catholics deeply committed to Jesus to enlist in the church's civil service, that is, to become paraprofessionals or mini-priests or mini-sisters as ministers or deacons....The work of the paraprofessional is, of course, an honorable calling....But when it is presented to the public in print, in parish budgets, in pastoral letters, or in the media as the model for all rank-and-file Catholics, a non-nutritious theology is being dispensed.[2]

The writer of these words gives some examples. He logically takes to task a Chicago journalist who worked for the *Chicago Tribune* and decided at thirty-four to become a Benedictine monk, saying that off and on he had been thinking of consecrating his life to God and had a need to get in touch with God again. These are noble sentiments, but ones that put down all the rest of the people "out there" who are thereby made to feel less committed, less holy, less in touch. He chastises the popular spiritual writer Henri Nouwen for the same reason. Henri spoke of his father, who told him to do well in school, and his mother, who told him that what's really important is that he love Jesus. So he became a priest. Again, the impression is that the two—school and loving Jesus—are incompatible.

The point is that we need to appreciate that there are indeed diverse and separate charisms but that *all* are responsible for building up both church and world. There should be no artificial split, as if the church and the world were opposed or never would meet. When you build one, you build the other. There is, of course, a question of emphasis and the priest's role is crucial to the unity within the community, but nevertheless all are on mission. In a word, shared responsibility must include the renewal of the secular order. We must acquire an integrative vision of the unity of the secular and the sacred. Or, as we would say in our tradition, a sharper sacramental sense. Our slogan should be not secular or sacred, but celebrated and experienced.

Still, it's not easy. As the working paper of the National Center for the Laity expressed it:

The task of integrating faith with secular life has become more complex. As "new" Catholics, we faced different questions than those which confronted earlier generations. How do we exercise power, wealth and influence responsibility? Has our sense of stewardship kept pace with our increasing economic and social status? What is the relationship between our work and our faith?...Our task is made more difficult by the tendency among many members of our church, both clerical and lay, to legitimize as religious only the work of church professionals and to ignore or downgrade the work that Catholics do in the world.

We spend most of our waking hours and energies doing the work of the world: rearing families, shouldering the responsibilities of our professions and occupations, and participating in the social, cultural and political life of our neighborhoods and communities. Our challenge is to take responsibility for humanizing the secular world by discovering the religious meaning embedded in these experiences.[3]

Hence, as we said in the last chapter, the need for support

groups and spiritual direction. And, here also, we might add, is the need for a critical understanding of the role of the priest:

> While preaching and presiding, priests must surely be aware that attitudes to moral values and social issues will be educated and developed in the hearing of God's word and through a deepened understanding of the meaning of the sacramental rites and symbols through which Christ is present in the body of the faithful....None of the other activities that a priest now engages in will bear much fruit if the sacramental assembly is not a place where the Christian people can deepen their sense of being God's people, and their sense of mission which they have as such a people in the society in which they belong.... While recent church teaching insists on the difference between order and baptism, it continually speaks of priestly ministry as a service to the priesthood of the baptised. Priestly service empowers the baptised to discover the presence of Christ in their lives, to imitate him, and to testify to the reign of God in the midst of human doings.[4]

A final reflection: any challenge and sense of world mission, it seems to me, also demands a new perspective on ecumenism. If we are to learn not to define Catholic laity in the negative, we must also learn not to define others who are not Catholic in the negative. We should learn to stress the positive overall presence of God, and God's operative presence in *all* lives. We try to discern where God is also acting in the Jewish, Moslem, Hindu, and other communities and, to that extent, where we can collaborate on any project that promotes human values. Being a Catholic is not invalidated because others show the same qualities and virtues. Remember, being a Catholic is not to be unique in the sense of being singular; it is a way of seeing, of "catholic" or universal seeing, and learning. As a Jesuit priest in Nepal says, he has found a rich and beautiful dimension in the Hindu-Buddhist culture:

> The secular reductionist spirit of so much of Western cul-

ture is not yet the world in which most Nepalese live.... Here religion is not just my affair; it is our affair. This "our" also refers to the entire created order, for God is present in all creation, and all things have an individual and collective Dharma to fulfill....

To seek happiness outside the Dharma is at best futile, at worst damning. Leading the life of adharma (sin) not only hurts the individual but sets into motion ripples of action that affect the universe. All reality is interrelated, flowing from and returning to a common Source.[5]

Such words are reminiscent of our doctrine of the Vine and the Branches, the Mystical Body of Christ. Or of Alice Walker's Shug Avery in *The Color Purple* when she says:

One day when I was sitting quiet and feeling like a motherless child which I was, it come to me: that feeling of being part of everything, not separate at all. I knew that if I cut a tree, my arm would bleed. And I laughed and I cried and I run all around the house. I knew just what it was. In fact when it happen you can't miss it.

In the following chapters we're going to see how one parish tries to involve people and give them a sense of home, of community, of ownership. We're going to look at a lot of ideas that bond people into a common enterprise. We're going to assume many, many volunteers. But we will still insist that the purpose of the ideas and approaches, the purpose of the parish itself, is to empower and celebrate experience: the experience of being a Christian in the everyday world with its occupations and challenges and its daily revelations—for those who will see—of God.

PART TWO

Hands On

CHAPTER 5

Seven Pastoral Tasks: Three Cs

In the last chapter we saw the broad areas of concern for the pastor or pastoral minister. In this chapter and the next two we break down those concerns in a very practical way into what I call the Seven Tasks of the pastor or pastoral minister under the memory device of the "Seven Cs," three in this chapter and three in the next and one the final one by itself. Many translatable examples will be included.

1. *Concept.* This refers to your own concept of what church is, your own vision which, consciously or unconsciously, you will act on. Included in that vision must be a sense that the church in reality has a double face: that of Magisterium and that of Mystery. The magisterium is the institutional side, necessary for existence, a bulwark against error and wind-blown

reeds, rooted in the apostolic mandate itself. The mystery is the lived side, the experienced "sacramental" side, the everyday epiphanies of falling in love, teaching a class, hugging, being accepted, running through autumn leaves, forgiveness, surprise, integrity, imagination, and moral dignity.

If you're exclusively into the magisterium-institutional side, you'll try to get people "into the church," and obedience is the final criterion. If you're exclusively into the mystery side, you'll try to get people to pause and adore where they are, and freedom is the final criterion. Both can go to excess, but both are needed and only one side or the other is heresy. Actually, most people are in-between: they appreciate the institutional side of the church but it's relatively unimportant to them. Their pastor is more significant to them than the pope, the local mayor than the bishop, the parish council than the synod, the neighborhood than the Vatican, and baptism more than ordination.

People see the church as a kind of two-tier arrangement. Or, if you want a metaphor, the church is like a Maypole—a straight pole stuck firmly in the ground with ribbons strung from the top and people grasping the other ends and dancing wildly around it. The magisterium-institutional side is the pole itself. It is firm, rooted, stable and will fall only to the great harm of all. The mystery side is the long, long ribbons waving in the breeze, waiting to be grasped for life's dance. Now there are two groups of people gathered here. There is one group huddled around the pole propping it up and devoting its energies to its care and protection. (And this usually requires that their backs are to the rest of the world.) There is another group, appreciative of the pole, but only peripherally acknowledging it because (1) the pole's a long, long way off and (2) they're too busy with the dance and if the pole doesn't like some of the steps, that's too bad. Anyway, if the distant pole starts to spin and whirl in order to reel in the flowing ribbons, some will let go altogether. And if the pole won't bend and give a little the dancers will get angry or feel stifled. But if, on the other hand, the dancers disdain the pole and walk away from it, they run the danger of losing their moorings or winding up dizzy, dancing to a tune that ultimately says nothing to them.

Eugene Kennedy explains the difference by his use of the First (Maypole) and Second (ribbons) Cultures in the church:

> Second Culture Catholics do not hold their breath when a Synod of Bishops is held in Rome; they do not care much about who may succeed to some archiepiscopal vacancy in a powerful city...do not follow the strictly ecclesiastical "news" whose buzz can be heard constantly in the pillared halls of the First Culture....Nor do they feel that their religious fervor or belief is tested by whether they side with either the Vatican or its critics....For them Catholicism is a way of life, and they have enough to do managing the problems of their everyday existence....They look to the church for support in carrying out their responsibilities to their families, and, in the work force and the professions, they expect that the church can speak to them with wisdom and encouragement about the great moral issues of the day. They expect that the church will comprehend tragedy and joy and that it will stand with them in both.[1]

Pastoral ministers today must "see" both sides of this church and not mistake the one as wholly defining the other. So, what's your concept of church, particularly in its local parish expression? What do *you* see? Do you see the parish as a miniature Vatican or the gathering place of the People of God? Can you mediate official and street theology, the Tradition and the experience or, more critically, even be aware that that's what you must do because both are church? Are those worthy of your ministrations only those graced by Holy Orders and Matrimony, or are all called through common baptism of which the other sacraments are charisms?

Do you view the pastor as "pope-on-the-scene" or as a fellow pilgrim with the charism of both leading and learning from the community? Is he the "lone ranger" or a participant in the common venture of shared and collaborative ministry? Is the true witness and proclaimer only the pastor or gifted soul or the community as a whole? (In practice, do you individually instruct converts or does the community walk with them in the R.C.I.A. process?) Do you see that your task is not to challenge people to be in *or* out of the church, but rather to be in *and* out—that is, to gather and then to scatter with the Good News? Do you see their parish-churchy lives as the only validating indicator of spirituality, or do you see them "being church" in their lives as "Workers, Players and Lovers," at the office, at the stadium, in bed? With your concept of church, how would you build a building for it? What would the furniture, space, arrangement, and programs say about who and what they are? What voice would the people have and how responsible would they be—would they be *invited* to be—for the church planted in this time and place?

Finally, do you really believe that they are loyal? As much as one might be disturbed about some Catholics "doing their own thing," they really are loyal. Seven out of ten would almost never consider leaving the church. Forty-eight percent of Catholics say that the church is "the most important" or "among the most important" parts of life.[2] But remember, "church" to them is not the institutional side about which they really do not care all that much and from which they are distancing themselves. By church they mean the impact of Christ and his gospel on their own lives. In a word, as Andrew Greeley has well noted, they are loyal to the church that offers them the three elements that compel them to stay: (1) their Catholic heritage; (2) community in the parish; and (3) the "sacramentality of Catholicism" which "has tremendous appeal for the imaginative dimension of personality." The eucharist holds together all three components."[3] It's good to note all this since pastors and pastoral associates, trained as they are in management and administration, might overlook the basic sacramentality of their calling. All these are concept or vision questions and they demand much of the pastoral leader, especially in his or her spiritual and intellectual formation. So much depends on this first pastoral task that there's no ducking the answers—even silence will be a potent answer.

2. *Convey.* This second category indicates that we must teach or convey to the people who and what they are, coaxing and inviting them to be the People of God—and an adult People of God at that. This very much implies, of course, that you as pastor or pastoral leader must let go. Letting go translates into two realities. One, you must learn the "Glenmary Dance." The Glenmary Fathers, as you may know, move into priestless territories, stay to build a parish and native leadership, and then move on. The same could be true of our pastoral leaders. He or she must teach, show, practice, lead, and then move away. Let the people own the parish. I remember when I first introduced the liturgy of the hours (namely the morning office) as a means of showing the people alternate ways of public prayer besides the daily Mass (and, I might add, anticipating the time when they might have no priest). I did my homework, shared my learning, practiced the morning office, led it for a while, and then invited them to lead. So I literally went from the sanctuary to sitting in the front pew, then the center pew, then the back pew, and then I "danced" right out the front door. Now the people own this prayer and I attend or not as a participant.

Second, you must not only convey who and what they are; it is imperative that you *give them the sources*. They must know chapter and verse, so to speak, of the New Testament, the Vatican II and subsequent documents, and pertinent themes in the Revised Code of Canon Law (which for the first time has many of their rights spelled out). They must be sure of their ground, have access to the sources, and know they are in tune with the teaching church. (Such knowledge also protects them from any regressive whims of a new pastor. It's unfortunate to have to say that, but it's necessary because often dioceses do not have a common vision.) Not that everyone has to be in the same place at the same time, but an overall and secure diocesan commitment to renewal at least helps you feel that you're part of a team (a chronic lack, for priests), on a common journey, while making room for dissenters. Too often, there is no firm overall diocesan vision or philosophy. Then the problem is that you know what you're doing is fundamentally idiosyncratic and personal and you get that sinking feeling that all could be changed when you leave. It's very demoralizing fearing that you'll be undone, not by a reactionary successor, but by an unarticulated and uncommitted vision from up top.

❏ Pastor's Luncheon. I have a form letter that I send to certain people asking them to gather two to four other people, Catholic or non-Catholic, parishioners or not, that I will treat to lunch at a local restaurant. As part of the letter says: "In exchange for the treat, I just want to chitchat, pick the brains of the group, hear their thoughts and (I'm not above it) listen to local gossip." It's a way to keep in touch with what's going on.

❏ No-Strings Education. The parish has a policy that whenever a good workshop or seminar comes up the pertinent people are invited to attend with all expenses paid (where the money comes from, in case you're wondering, we'll see later on). This keeps them current and, as a result, keeps the parish current as well. Furthermore, each spring, when all those notices come out announcing a few hundred summer courses and workshops, the parish will publicize about 15 or 20 of them that are reasonably nearby. Anyone interested is free to attend, again with the parish picking up expenses. But the "no-strings" phrase is critical because that means that there really are no strings attached. The people don't have to come back to report or perform or commit to anything. The course or workshop is purely a gift. Because summer is high vacation time, no more than 10 to 15 people might actually take advantage of this offer. But think it over: 10 or 15 people multiplied by 15 years I've been here equals some 100 to 150 parishioners who have sat at the feet of a Ray Brown or a Sandra Schneiders or a Lucien Deiss. They've *got* to be affected, got to form a kind of educated and inspired underground that raises the general tone of the parish. No-strings education is a long-range benefit.

3. *Create Climate.* This is probably the most important of the Seven Cs. It's difficult to pin down, but let's put some flesh

and bones on it by looking at three practical categories.

A. The pastor or pastoral minister must create a climate of *freedom*. This is a freedom to do, to experiment (my usual reply to suggestions, even those I'm wary of, is to say, "try it, let's see where it goes"), to make mistakes, to gather and associate (that's why we have no stipends for weddings, baptisms, funerals, the use of the hall or facilities etc; to gather in worship or celebration is the people's right, not a privilege to be paid for), and, most practical of all, to know what tools are needed and *where things are*. The mysteries of the heating and air conditioning systems, the location of chairs, tables, coffee, cups, urns, napkins, table cloths, toilet paper, stationery, stamps, and light switches should not be hidden within the recesses of the Trinity or confined to a few members of the hierarchical clique. All this should be public knowledge—with the implicit freedom that goes with such knowledge. In our parish every door, switch box, and wall has full information pasted on it. (Also, unwisely for most places, every door is open twenty-four hours a day, so keys are never a problem). People should have full access to their property and all within it and should not have to ask either for permission to assemble (beyond the necessities of scheduling) or go begging for simple amenities. Full access is important. Anything less is not only demeaning but sends a message of dependency and power that was alien to Jesus, who saw authority not as lording it over others but as service.

B. The pastor or pastoral minister must create a climate of *trust*.

❑ We have a tithing committee. The parish as a whole tithes ten percent of its total annual income. One third of the amount goes to international charities, another third to national charities, and the final third to local charities. The tithing committee investigates and distributes the money—with the total trust of the parish.

❑ People of the parish take turns (after some instruction and guidance) in writing the Prayers of the Faithful; many of them are profound and touching and they are not censored beforehand.

❑ People are completely free to purchase what they need. If they have a job to do, they have full freedom to buy what they need without prior permission and send the bill to the parish. We trust them and they have not abused this. Since money is power, this is a strong symbol of trust.

❑ The parish has a red pickup truck. The keys are always in it. People who need it to transport furniture or food to the needy or for any real need, are free to come and take it. We trust they will not abuse it.

❑ In the kitchen off our parish hall we have about twenty pigeon holes for mail slots. People who do things around the parish are free to have mail sent in their name to the parish address and we put it into their slot.

C. The pastor or pastoral minister must create a climate of *responsibility*. If the people are the church, then they have responsibilities—here's some areas that they take care of:

❑ Lent and Advent packet. Every Advent and Lent the parish sends out a packet of things to do to make the seasons holy. We have three big boxes marked "Advent," "Lent," and "ideas." People all through the year—and the staff who tend to get all those multitudinous seasonal flyers—drop ideas into the appropriate boxes. As the liturgical seasons approach, several families (recruited before the parish year starts) empty the box on a table, pick and discuss what they would like to receive in a packet and then give their findings to the office, which then orders and mails out to all the parishioners the material they've chosen.

❑ Bulletin Board. On the back wall of the church we have fixed a large bulletin board. On this bulletin board, every six to eight weeks (or at seasonal times), a volunteer (a different one from year to year) makes a display of photographs (we take a lot of pictures of our many activities), cutouts, and text that show something of parish life. People like to see themselves, the display is attractive, and the changing keeps things fresh and novel.

❑ Christmas Decoration. I would venture to say that most parishes have the same few people decorate the church each year and they've been doing it since World War I. And don't you dare move a poinsettia! In our parish we have a different neighborhood decorate the church each year (again, recruited during the post-Easter season when we begin to plan our parish year: people will agree to anything months ahead of time—and then panic as it nears!). You run the risk of having the church turn out looking like a department store (hasn't happened yet), but that's the risk. This whole venture has, I think, a great deal of symbolism. First, it involves a whole neighborhood, parents, grandparents, teens, children, singles, etc. Second, it gives them pride and ownership and you can hear the kids coming into church pointing out which ornament they placed on the large tree. Third, it breaks the monopoly of the same people always doing the same thing and who often, by their very competence, unwittingly close out other people, other talent. Fourth, it's another opportunity for trust, responsibility, and ownership.

❑ Bread Baking. People, men as well as women, bake our large altar bread. There's someone in charge of keeping the supply fresh. One woman told me how much it meant to her and her family to see the bread they baked used for the eucharist.

❑ Guest Book. In our church foyer we have a large ledger. Visitors are invited to sign their name and address and make any comments they wish. To every legible name and address is sent a letter by those responsible for the task in a given year, usually shut-ins. Here's a copy of the letter:

Dear Friends:
In our vestibule as you enter our church in Colts Neck, New Jersey, is a Guest Book. You were gracious enough to sign it and this correspondence is to thank you for doing so.

We hope you enjoyed your visit. We think, of course, that our buildings and grounds are beautiful and that our parish spirit is great. That you were both able to share this for a while and even add to it is a cause for joy and gratitude. So we thought that we would write to tell you how appreciative we are.

Do drop by again, and once more, thanks for gracing us with your visit.

Sincerely yours in the Lord,
Kathryn Crine and Jane McGuire,
Hospitality

❑ One-on-One. Many years ago when a woman was about to have a mastectomy, she came to me for counseling. Then one day when it was all over and she was herself again, she thanked me for my help and said, "By the way, if anyone ever has this problem, feel free to give her my name. I'll be glad to talk to her." That's when it hit me. I knew a good number of "closet" sufferers who had worked through some difficult times. So I went and asked each of them if they would go public and give their name and phone number for contact. Thus was born our "One-to-One Ministry." In our parish booklet the introduction to this ministry goes like this:

"Bear one another's burdens," St. Paul has told us. And there is no one who can bear another's burdens, troubles, problems, and hardships as someone who has been there before you. Therefore, in the spirit of deep Christian love and courage, the people whose names are listed here all have personal experience (and expertise) in the categories mentioned. They are "wounded healers" ready to listen and help in the name of the Lord.

Then are listed categories (with names and phone numbers) from adoption to terminal illness.

These are all very practical examples of how we can create a climate of freedom, trust, and responsibility. All of our actions are symbolic and reveal our understanding and priorities. That's why it's not what we say, not our fine mission statements, not our easy phrases of "community" and "People of God" that count. That's Elisa Doolittle stuff. She and we want something more: "Show me!" And, of course, implicit in all this, is the challenge to our own sense of identity and needs and control and the personal spirituality that can imitate Jesus the footwasher.

CHAPTER 6

Three More Cs

Here we continue with three more Cs as part of our Seven Pastoral Tasks.

4. *Connect.* One of the more pleasant as well as critical tasks of the pastor or pastoral minister is to connect people. Because we tend to have an overview, we can reach out and bring together on a project people who don't know one another, or at least not well. The process is what I call "cross pollination." That's why I seldom if ever call for volunteers. We all know that we can write down the names of those who will respond before we ever send out the word. The trouble with calling for volunteers (all the time, not sometimes) is that you get the same competent people, and you preempt others who might never come forward knowing the territory is already spoken for, or worse, will allow a "let-George-do-it" attitude to take over. Rather, my procedure is to invite. I send a personal letter

saying we need help. The pastor or pastoral assistant still has enough mystique to command a response. People don't like to say no to "Father" or whoever's in charge. But beyond this, deliberately inviting unmet parishioners is a way to connect and build community, to provide the forum whereby people might get to meet and know one another.

Asking advice also falls under this heading. Whenever we have a really serious project at hand, besides getting the advice of the parish council, I always invite, by personal letter, perhaps 10 or 15 groups of 30, people across the board from every segment of the parish. I ask for their input and advice, get them talking, and let them hear from others they might not ordinarily hear from. Besides being helpful, it connects.

5. *Convoke.* This, I suppose, is an aspect of creating the climate. We convoke or gather people first of all for liturgy. People have their various tasks from ushering to lecturing. The presider does just that: presides and brings "holy order" to the variety of people participating. But hospitality, too, is an aspect of convoking the people. The doors must be open to community needs. Looking over our parish booklet I find such groups meeting at the parish as AA, Al-anon, GA (Gamblers Anonymous), Senior citizens, Alienated Catholics, Polaris (Young adults), "Mopits" (stands for Mothers of Preschoolers, Infants, Toddlers, and School age children), Scripture sharing groups, etc.

6. *Cult.* This means that ritual is very important. It's the imagination's hold on truth. It reaches people in ways that words cannot. Joseph Campbell, the great mythologist, told Bill Moyers that "Preachers err by trying to talk people into belief; better they reveal the radiance of their own discovery," and that is usually done by sign and symbol. Campbell comments on how Jesus had the "eye": "What a magnificent reality he saw in the mustard seed."[1] Think of all those people who come from all over the galaxy to get ashes. Much as we might make fun of them (the once-a-yearers who would never think of approaching the eucharist) there is something resonant about the ashes that's compelling—and palms, incense, bells,

dance, movement, gesture, and all the rest.

As Catholics, we seem to have let go of our incredible heritage of ritual and symbol that carried dark and exciting meanings too deep for words. Ironically, it is science today that, confronting the mysteries of physics, is reaching desperately for mystical, symbolic language and sign to identify the unidentifiable, to name the unnamable. So we should never underestimate the power of symbol and ritual and what they can mean to the parish. Here are some ways, from the silly to the serious, that we use in our parish.

We presume that most parishes celebrate all sacraments before and with the community. There are three things we add.

❏ As the baptism ceremony draws to a close, I ask who is the oldest person in the congregation. Someone might raise his or her hand and say "72" and I'll kid and say "I hear 72, is there anyone 73?" until we get to the (admitted) oldest, who's say, 76. So it's 76 once, twice, and gone. Then we turn serious and ask that person to come and lay his or her hands on the newly baptized in a physical gesture of passing on the (faith) tradition. It is a very moving moment.

❏ Then we ask the parents to speak to the congregation and tell what they wish for their newly baptized child. What do they want most of all for his or her future?

❏ At the end of Mass, during the meditation time after Communion, we read a letter to the congregation. The letter is addressed to the newly baptized child with the instructions typed on the envelope that it not be opened until that child is about to make his or her confirmation. Here is the letter:

Dear _____,

When you were born, your parents thought so much of you that they wanted to share the most precious gift they had: their faith.

So they approached the Christian community at St. Mary's, Colts Neck, New Jersey, and asked the people if they would be willing to have a new member; and would they be willing to create the climate within which you could and would grow to know and love Jesus Christ.

The community said yes and so on_____ you and your parents and godparents, family and friends came to St. Mary's. There at the twelve o'clock Mass, in full view of the congregation, you were inserted into the Christian family.

The people were happy and they applauded you afterwards. And then your parents brought you home and had a celebration there, too, because of this joyful event.

That was many years ago. Now you are ready to complete your initiation into the Christian faith through the sacrament of confirmation. You are now ready to speak for yourself and declare yourself a Catholic and your desire to bear witness to the gospel in your life.

We hope that this letter finds you ready and willing to do so—as we hope that the years past have given you comfort and joy in the Lord.

Signing this letter are your pastor at that time, Father Bausch, Sister Stella, and the other names on the back of this paper, names of the people from the congregation present when you were baptized and who first welcomed you into our midst.

Today, as you read this letter before you are confirmed, remember this: we still welcome you, pray for you, hope for you, and, through the years and distance, love you.

Sincerely yours in Christ,

Before Mass, members of the prebaptismal committee have gone around church collecting signatures on the back of the letter. The letter is then sealed inside the envelope and presented to one of the parents.

❑ A final baptismal ritual is the anniversary card. On the first anniversary of the child's baptism we send an attractive card (of course, someone's in charge of this; we had the cards printed up professionally so that they would look good), something like an invitation with a clip art baptismal scene on the front and when you open the card the text inside reads:

Happy First Anniversary!
One year ago this week, your baby was welcomed into the Christian community of St. Mary's. The event was, you recall, a lovely rite of entrance into the People of God who, overjoyed with a new member, applauded.
We just want to wish you a happy first anniversary of this baptism day, along with the promise of our prayers that your parenting, by word and example, continues to connect your child with this community and continues to draw the little one closer to the source of all life.
The People of St. Mary's, Colts Neck, N.J.

So there you are: a laying on of hands, a wish from the parents, a letter for the future, and an anniversary remembrance. None of them is that important, but connected to a time of joy and the rituals of initiation, they all form a continuing ritual that will remain longer than words.

❑ Ceremony of Departure. If we have significant rituals for new life, renewed life (reconciliation), blended life (marriage), eternal life (Christian burial), then we should have something for those families or individuals who move away from the parish, especially for those for whom the parish has meant a great deal. So we have a brief Ceremony of Departure. We ask the family to come up to the sanctuary after the homily and face the congregation.

Presider (addressing the congregation): My dear friends, the _____ family is departing from our midst. We have known and loved them. They have journeyed with us and now they move on. We shall miss them, but we also know that they shall carry the spirit of St. Mary's wherever they go.
Our prayers follow them and so I ask you all to kneel for the moment for a brief litany to which you are to reply, "Lord be with them."

Holy Father, give them vision and strength,
Glorious Son, show them the way,
Loving Spirit, surprise them with joy,
Holy Angels, surround them,
Saints of God, protect them,
Root them in your holy love,
Send them to plant the faith,
Make them witnesses of your truth,
Be their newness,
Be their adventure,
Be their laughter,
Be their memory,
Be their courage.
O God, you know that we shall miss the _____
family, but we also know that you always send forth your
people to new places, jobs, and tasks so that the gospel
may be spread and your people may witness in all places
to the wonders of your love. Comfort us with memories
of them. Encourage them with memories of us. We ask
this through Christ our Lord. Amen.

Then we give them a gift, usually a framed photograph of
the church. The person or persons are invited to say goodbye
and to express what the community has meant to them and
then the whole congregation stands as we sing our (now) traditional "Blessing Aaron." This might take only six or seven
minutes, but even with the evident parish chauvinism, it is a
ritual that is touching and meaningful to all.

❑ The Blessing of the Food Carriers. On the last Sunday of
each month the people bring food and paper goods for the
poor and place their packages in the sanctuary. At the end of
the main Mass we have representatives of the various parish
ministries (plus general parishioners) come up before the final
blessing. The little folder the presiders (and those carrying the
food) has reads as follows:

Presider: (just before final dismissal): The community calls
              from its midst representatives to carry the do-

nated food to the Sharing Shed.

(People step forward—men and women, boys and girls selected by the committee at the beginning of Mass—pick up a bag of food, and turn and face the congregation)

Presider: Let us pray. Almighty God, Lover of the Poor and Friend of the outcast, bless those who gave this food from the goodness of their hearts. Bless too the hands that will distribute and the hands that will receive.

And may all of us know that we have no right to pride for, as disciples of the Lord and servants of one another, we are but doing our duty, beholden as we are to the gospel of Our Lord Jesus Christ. Amen.

(Here the presider sprinkles the carriers with holy water and then he announces to the congregation)

This Mass is ended. Let us go to love and serve the Lord.

All: Thanks be to God

(The carriers process out behind the acolytes and in front of the presider. They go directly out the front door and up to the Sharing Shed to deposit the food on the shelves.)

All this, this witnessing ritual of concern, takes about four or five minutes.

❏ The Sharing Shed. This a large garage-like building that the people of the parish built. It has shelves for food and poles and shelves for clothing as well as two freezers for frozen meals. The shed is open every Saturday from 10:00 to 2:00 and Tuesdays from 4:00 to 5:00 (that's our CCD day, so help is available). No clothing is accepted except twice a year (to prevent crowding), with the exception of infant and baby clothes (always needed). Large furniture is not accepted (space would soon disappear) but we act as agents by keeping a card file of large furniture for those who need it. There is an emergency number to call. All this is printed on a large sign attached to the shed. Our Samaritan ministry is in charge and rotates hours. Likewise, to prevent a glut of the same item, we have asked the people to concentrate on the items under the first letter of their last name. Thus:

A-F	G-K	L-P
canned vegetables	canned meats	dry milk
pasta	canned fish	dry cereal
macaroni & cheese	spaghetti sauce	muffin mix
noodles	canned stew	pancake mix
Hamburger/Tuna helper		Bisquick

Q-U	V-Z
towels, napkins	Jello
cleaning materials	cake mixes
face soap	canned fruit
canned juices	any desserts
condiments	

❑ Halloween. On Halloween everyone who comes to morning worship comes in costume and liturgy is followed by a party. It may seem outrageous, but behind masks and gowns are the more serious symbols connecting us with life and death, with the world of the supernatural, with that deep Catholic sense of being on a common journey with all those who have gone before, are now, and are to come. All Hallows' Eve, All Saints, All Souls—they're all there.

❑ The Communal Confessions. The format is similar to that in many other parishes. We have an opening hymn and prayer, a scripture reading and homily followed by silent time, and a public examination of conscience involving a reader asking reflective questions of the congregation. When it comes time to celebrate the sacrament of reconciliation, the priests, who were sitting in the sanctuary by the presiding chair, come down and stand before the front pews. The people place their stoles over their heads and then the priests sit at chairs placed around the sanctuary. All lights are put out. The automatic slide projector, already set up, is turned on. Meditative slides are shown on the screen behind the altar while background music (a record) is played. All is in darkness except two candles on a stand in the body of the church. Each person comes for one-on-one confession. As each finishes, he or she is handed a small candle. (A box of candles is beside each priest.) The people take the candle and light it from one of those two candles. The symbolism is powerful. Little by little, as each one completes the sacrament, the church moves from darkness to light. The slides occupy the people yet to come or who have come. The music makes nice background sounds and protects the confidentiality of the penitents who are confessing before the assembly up front before the priests.

When all are reconciled and the projector and music are turned off, there is a prayer, a sign of peace, and the recitation of the Our Father. Then, the church lights are put on, candles extinguished, and a final prayer and hymn are sung. Then there are refreshments in the hall. If it should happen that there are too few priests for the crowd (we usually get around 300 to 400 people) then we will follow the same procedure but cut off the penitential lines ten minutes before closing with the option that the priests will return to church after the ceremony for anyone who wishes to come back. The idea is to keep the ceremony within a reasonable hour. Of course, if no priests show up to help, we will have General Absolution. Then in place of the slides and candles we will have some congregational action, for example, having the people come down the aisle and dip their hands into the baptism font, or coming in procession to insert little wooden crosses (we've made from popcicle sticks) into a large styrofoam cross we have.

❏ Other "movements" throughout the year are: (1) having those to be confirmed and those who make first communion always come up, dip their hand into the baptismal font (which is in our front center aisle), and bless themselves in place of being sprinkled as a way of showing the unity of the initiation sacraments; (2) having permanent photographs hanging around the church as a way of celebrating and affirming our communal life; (3) giving small round loaves of bread to people as they leave the Holy Thursday liturgy.

We'll mention more items in the course of this book, but these are here as illustrations of the power of "cult," of celebrating the mysteries of salvation in ritual symbol and metaphor that speak to people in deep and resonant ways. This all means, of course, that the imagination of the pastoral minister is at least as critical as his or her theological formation.

CHAPTER 7

The Final Task:
Change and Challenge

Change. This is the seventh and final "C." Since it is important and needs a bit more explanation we have this brief chapter about it. This concern about change means that the pastoral minister by definition is an agent of change. By this I don't mean that someone walks into a parish with an agenda to change everything. That's guaranteed to mobilize the mob for a lynching. No, I mean that in these days the pastoral minister not only symbolizes change but in fact must mediate those changes in ministry and spirituality that are already taking place. The people—and the clergy—need a great deal of help here.

A word about change itself. Some may know the work of the futurist Joel Barker who bases his work on that of Thomas

Kuhn (author of *The Structure of Scientific Revolutions*).[1] Kuhn set out to discover why scientists often overlooked or turned down now-famous scientific breakthroughs and discoveries. He found that often scientists had such preconceived and pre-set mind patterns that those patterns actually screened out other ways of seeing and doing. The habit patterns of the mind precluded doing or seeing things any other way and so the scientists could not accept any far out or "bizarre" or unusually different patterns—or, as Kuhn calls them, paradigms. Such paradigms, he maintains, are strongly held rules and regulations that act as filters and screen information coming into one's mind. We all see the world through such paradigms so much so that what may seem perfectly obvious for someone with one paradigm may be totally imperceptible for someone else with another paradigm.

For example, I remember years ago in psychology class that one of the common examples was to look at what seemed to be an upside-down vase but which was actually a bug the natives considered a delicacy. We students saw a vase because the bug was simply outside our paradigm, while the native saw a delicious tidbit because a vase was outside his paradigm. Or, there's the example that Kuhn and Barker use. About twenty years ago the Swiss had almost 80 to 85 percent of the market on watches. Precision and craftsmanship were their hallmarks. Today, Switzerland has only 18 percent of the watch market. Who has the biggest market? Yes, the Japanese. The irony is that it was a Swiss watchmaker who came in with an entirely new concept: the digital watch powered not by precision springs and movements but by a battery. However, so ingrained was the old paradigm of making watches with springs and movements that the Swiss could not see anything else working and so, unfortunately (for them), they did not bother either to pursue or to patent the new process.

At an international watch convention the Swiss had a minor, out-of-the-way display of the digital watch lost among the standard watches. A man from Texas Instruments and a Japanese happened to notice it and, as they say, the rest is history.

The point was that the Swiss mindset, the paradigm, was so filtering that it could not allow a new and radical pattern in. Be it noted, by the way, that people with different paradigms, like the man who came up with the digital, battery-powered watch, are usually "on the edge" people, kind of outsiders who see things differently—and who may be creatively right or tragically wrong (Jesus would fit in here).

So it is obvious that we will run into conflict in this era of our church. The undeniable fact is that we are in the tensions of changing paradigms. The concept of ministry is changing. The shift from the centrality of ordination to that of baptism-confirmation as the basis of ministry is taking place. The spirituality of the past with its first Fridays, novenas, weekly confessions, and a basically monastic coloring, quite the preserve of the religious and clergy (as we have seen), is giving way to marketplace spirituality, to the universal call to holiness. The model of the sole leader (bishop or priest) doing it all is giving way to shared and collaborative ministry. No one needs to be reminded that we are in a midst of change.

And it's a change charged with resistance. Change threatens that to we which we have become accustomed and people—bishops, priests, laity—are all among the resisters. Why resist? Besides the natural conflict of paradigms—the movement mindset versus the digital mindset—the four most common reasons why people resist change are:

1. A desire not to lose something of value. Certainly a legitimate fear. Priests, for example, may have so connected churchy activity with their personal role that if someone else reads the scripture, gives out Communion, visits the sick, or shares in decision making, the value and indeed existence of their very self-identity is severely threatened.

2. A misunderstanding of the change and its implications. As a pastor or pastoral minister, I may have to approach ministry more as a servant than an overlord. I may have to remove the altar rail which separates priest and people, the secular and the sacred—and what will happen if it all gets blurred and mixed up?

3. A belief that the change does not make sense for me. Resistance here will take the form of passive aggression. I will boldly say the rosary during the preparation hymn.

4. A low tolerance for change because change requires new skills and new behavior. Perhaps my whole training has been that of manager who gives orders. I don't have listening skills.

Of course, as difficult as it is for individuals to change, it is far more difficult for organizations to change. Organizations are by definition conservative in the best sense: conserving real values from the past. They tend towards stability and that's surely a big appeal in a fast-paced world and accounts, I think, for some of the appeal of fundamentalism. On the other hand, one of the hazards of organizations is that ways of doing things do tend to harden into procedures and rules and codes. "That's the way we do things are here." Efficiency often subverts effectiveness. We are doing it well, but what are we doing? It's often the "on-the-edge" people who ask embarrassing questions about this.

Getting back to our point: it is obvious that the pastoral minister is a critical change agent (and, as I said before a very symbol of clashing paradigms; after all, your job probably did not exist in the church ten or twenty years ago.) Accordingly, some of the questions he or she has to come to terms with are:

1. What are some of the ministry paradigms that have guided us in the past in the church? Do we understand (and are we sympathetic to) them?

2. As we look to the future, what new paradigms are being born, are needed? Do we understand *them*?

3. What opportunities do we have to develop new ministry paradigms?

4. What obstacles do we face in developing new paradigms?

5. What resources do we have to help us? (Workshops, facilitators, books, etc.)

So here we are, whether clergy or laity, confronted with a task of mediating change in a changing church and searching for ways of doing it and hopefully using compassion as our entry point of encounter. Anyway, as we wrestle with these questions, here are some guidelines in coming to terms with change:

1. Remember, the establishment of the change is not an end in itself. We don't go around proving how liberal we are by changing just for the sake of change. Change must be rooted in the tradition, authenticated by the church and guided by the best minds and hearts.

2. Introduce the change to a small group. This is always wise. Some good education with a small and receptive group is a good way to test the changes and hone your approach to a larger group.

3. Carefully consider the real losses that will result; allow people to talk about and especially to grieve over them. This is a kindly and healing thing to do. After all, there *are* losses and often some genuine good gets plowed under. Be sensitive to this.

4. Allow for as much flexibility as possible. Don't force an either-or situation. Either you take part in the liturgical dance or you wear the green scapular. Why not room for both? It's a big church. We should never make anyone feel that he or she is somehow less a Catholic, less a faith community member for the position he or she takes. (Remember, compassion is the point of entry.)

5. Build in an evaluation system. Establish beforehand the criteria for judging the success or failure of the change.

6. Look for win/win situations; minimize win/lost situations. We're all in this together.

I suppose that of all the " Seven Cs"—Concept, Convey, Climate, Connect, Convoke, Cult, and Change—the last might be the most challenging for the pastoral minister, not only because it is so difficult but also because it involves our own deepest movements, our own progress, our own letting go and moving into a Spirit-filled spirituality. The demands of integrating the polarities of our own lives are at stake or, if you will, forming new paradigms that include: power/powerlessness, youth/aging, action/contemplation, leadership/servanthood, hierarchy/collaboration. Perhaps, therefore, we can end with a few encouraging words from somebody who's been there, John Henry Cardinal Newman: "In a higher world it is otherwise; but here below to live is to change, and to be perfect is to have changed often."

CHAPTER 8

Council, Covenant, and Conscience

The Parish Council. I'm not going to discuss either the worth or benefit of parish councils. I take for granted that they are both worthy and beneficial and there are many successful models. I just want to share one model. My experience has been that most parish councils are (1) too large; (2) too "professional," that is, made up of some very competent people in their fields but whose sense of church might not match their secular expertise; (3) too disproportionate, that is, the council might spend two hours on the janitor's salary and ten minutes on the liturgy, and (4) too unbalanced, that is, in the light of the last remark, the finance committee might wag the whole thing.

To overcome some of these difficulties, we have structured

our parish council on a two-tiered model, or in two matching parts. One tier or part is called the parish assembly. The assembly consists of all the heads of every ministry and organization. They meet with members of the second tier or part, the parish council itself, every other month. The purpose of the meeting is to (1) issue written reports of activities since the last meeting, including the agenda and minutes of the parish council—everyone present gets a copy—plus any oral reports or commentary; (2) keep everyone abreast of what every other ministry is doing so we all have an overview of where we're going corporately; (3) mention adjustments in the calendar or activities that have to be made; and (4) let people lobby to their hearts' content for whatever they want. There are about 35 to 45 people present who make up this parish assembly. The agenda is the four points just listed and so the meeting never lasts more than two hours and you can count on an evening from 8:00 to 10:00. But, most of all, none of these people can vote. They are the doers and shakers, informers and lobbists. When we leave we know what's happening parishwide and what each other's programs are, their successes and failures. And we know their needs.

The second tier, the parish council, is made up of those *ex officio* persons as required by our diocese: pastor, associate(s), deacon(s), and the diocesan pastoral council delegate. The other six people are those who have been nominated by the parish at large (nominees must give their approval to have their names submitted) and then voted in by the parish council on a staggered roll-over basis. We decided not to have a direct popular election so we could control the geography and the sex balance. The two main duties of the parish council members are, first and foremost, *discernment* and then, only secondarily, voting. We're quite serious about this. The parish council is not to be stampeded into a quick vote. They must take time to discern (implying a certain church and parish sense), carefully and prayerfully, alone and corporately. The guiding and uppermost question is, "Is this of the gospel?" So many things come along that look so neat and sound so spiffy. Some projects and programs are really razzle-dazzle and smack of sure success. But we still stop and ask our question. We try to take the long view and keep discerning what we're in business for as a faith community. We're not the Kiwanis or the Rotary. We're a faith community. Will this or that make us a more viable sign of Christ? Can we resist the lure and glamor of "success" and keep our focus on who and what we are? Can we keep the gospel values straight?

The Holy Name or Altar-Rosary or even the Finance Committee doesn't have the last say. The vision does. This discernment model has proven (for us) a most happy one. Its very structure keeps pulling us back to our identity as a People of God. By the way, the parish council, as you can see, meets every month, one month by itself and the other month as part of the parish assembly. So the assembly people meet only six times a year and the council 12 times—not too great a demand. As the pastor, I have an equal vote and although by diocesan law the council is advisory, I abide by the majority decision. We have also agreed that if the council and I were ever seriously on opposite sides (this hasn't happened yet) we would appeal to outside arbitration and abide by that decision. Anyway, we find this model workable, comfortable (especially those short meetings), and practical in keeping us tied to the center of things.

The Covenant. You'll sense my conscience problem here, a not quite at-homeness, a struggle between compassion and challenge. Let me explain. It is quite clear that, through baptism, confirmation, and eucharist, one enters into a faith community. It's not just a negative matter of getting rid of original sin but also a positive matter of becoming a part of this pilgrim people, its traditions, saints, sinners, spirit, institutions, and celebrations. The Rite of Christian Initiation for Adults is reinforcing this communal journey, and the communal responsibility. Simply put, Christianity is not an individual religion; it is a communal one.

The challenge to this view is presented by the nominal Catholic, the cultural Catholic, the one for whom, communally (there is no judgment about his or her personal sanctity, which may be wonderful), there is all take and no give (coming around only for sacramental times). The dilemma is how to show compassion to these Catholics lest we risk the judgment of God (which actually I have less fear of; I'm more afraid of Andrew Greeley's judgment) and at the same time give them a challenge. After all, Christianity, as we said, is community with Jesus Christ as head. The sacraments are communal celebrations, the Mass is a communal celebration—can one, should one, treat them as individual drop-in times for personal needs? True, such nominal Catholics have histories, may have had bad experiences, been turned off by insensitive priests and all the rest. We must reach out to such inactive and alienated Catholics, but at the same time we shouldn't overromanticize them: there are those who are just indifferent with no desire to be anything more.

In any case, in our parish, instead of having newcomers, nominal or regular, just drop by the parish office and fill out a family information form, we give them a Covenant statement accompanied by a letter. The letter reads as follows:

Dear Friend,

One of our joys is to be able to welcome families like yours into our larger parish community. I hope you will be happy here and that the parish meets your expectations.

About four years ago the parish council voted to go beyond just collecting data on newly-registered families. They felt that since people are not in fact joining a church like some club, but rather are entering into a faith community with mutual rights and obligations, then we should perhaps talk more in terms of relationships. So they came up with the most solemn (and biblical) form of personal agreement and commitment, the Covenant.

So that's what you see enclosed here: a covenant between us and you, a signed agreement that we will be faithful and supportive to one another. I hope you won't be put off by it or offended in any way. But you know, seeking to enter this community is like any other relationship you have: you want and expect a give-and-take with the people of your life. All give with no return and all take with no giving is hurtful and eventually destructive to the relationship.

So with us. We are holding out a collective hand and we want you to grasp it. We are willing to bond ourselves to you in faith, hope, and love and we ask for the same from you. We promise fidelity. We ask fidelity. Fair enough.

So that's about it. This is all probably something very new for you, for in the old days you just joined a parish. Period. But, as they say, times have changed and we have grown more interested in having a real faith family than a registry of passive and inactive members.

Anyway, please read over the enclosed Covenant carefully and call me when you're ready to sign—which in itself is a nice excuse for me to meet you personally. This Covenant is temporary and we review it each year on the anniversary date.

So, once again, welcome. We are indeed thrilled to have you. We know that we can mutually enrich one another and look forward to a good (and godly) relationship. We await your call.

Meanwhile, much peace and blessing.

Sincerely yours in Christ,
Father Bausch

Forget that the letter is written for an educated audience (if you use the idea, you will of course modify it for your people) and notice several things. (1) The people are mildly surprised at this different approach and it gently puts them on notice about our serious intent to form a parish community; (2) we move immediately into relationship language, not institutional language; (3) we underscore the give-and-take of any relationship; (4) we put the brake on mere casualness about joining the parish; (5) we let them know that this is not a once-and-for-all deal, since the Covenant is reviewable and renewable, and (6) if they agree to sign the Covenant, we do get to meet them at their own homes and meet members of their families. We learn where they live and something about them. That part is very satisfying. By the way, people don't have to stop at the parish office or call. Our Welcome Wagon may contact them before that and leave them the Covenant packet.

(I might also mention that we have an extra edge in our favor. People are anxious to join the parish and we have a list of people waiting to join from other areas. This certainly heightens motivation and selectivity. Every year the parish council meets to consider applicants who have filled out a request sheet and we try to take as many as we can, given the space problems of CCD, potential marriages, proximity, etc. We give special consideration to young families. If they are in their 20s and 30s, with their children still going to church, we are willing to meet them more than halfway. We also benefit because this keeps a steady stream of young blood coming into the parish.)

On pages 92-93 there is the text of the Covenant, which is a folded, two-page, standard size document (so it can be put in a three-ring binder). The terms of the Covenant itself are on the first page, an explanation of it on the back of that. The next page of the covenant sheet contains the actual family information form and on the last, blank lines for any notes or remarks. The "Christian Service" listed in the Covenant itself can be chosen from our annual parish booklet that the people are given (more on the booklet later), and this service can be taken, a one-shot deal or something minor. It's the gesture that we're after. Very often the service puts new people into automatic contact with others and helps acclimate them to the community sooner.

So what are the minuses and pluses in our experience? The minuses might be an anxiety that we're coming on too hard, that some might find the whole notion of a covenant or contract distasteful, perhaps even un-Christlike, that in the hands

Date_____

_____
(Name of individual or family)
voluntarily wishes to enter into a preliminary

Covenant

with the community of St. Mary's, Colts Neck, New Jersey

These days, journeying with a particular faith-community is largely voluntary. There is no compulsion to choose this way of life or this parish. Rightly or wrongly, people do not attach any kind of mortal sin in missing Mass. Unbaptised infants are considered as going to heaven. There must be a reason, then, why freely and without such compulsions you are seeking to join this community. We presume that you are accordingly motivated by a desire both to give to and receive from this community: that as in any relationship, you are bonding yourself freely in the give-and-take of our common life.

Therefore, you are ready to enter into a covenant with us— that most solemn contract of mutuality, concern and shared responsibility. There is no requirement to be perfect or without flaw or sin; only the promise to be faithful. Accordingly, this Covenant states as follows:

I/we promise to walk faithfully with our fellow parishioners of St. Mary's, to worship with them regularly and to make some committment of Christian service, however temporary, as described in the Parish Booklet.

My/our Christian service is _____

Signed _____

Pastor/Associate _____

Parish Council

President/delegate _____

Witness _____

In due time you, and/or your family, along with other families, will be welcomed publicly and joyously into the community at one of the weekend Masses.

Explanation

1. A single name or the family name will go on the blank line.

2. Discuss and pray over the Covenant with your family. When you're ready, call the office (780-2666) and one of the staff will visit you.

3. The one obvious fact today is that current culture no longer supports a religious way of life, much less a Catholic way. This means that now you deliberately and willingly have to make a personal choice: Do I want to travel with this people or not? Do I want to give, contribute, be faithful with and to them? Do I and my family intend to be a genuine and full part of this faith community?

4. Worshipping regularly with the community means just that: every weekend (or most) celebrating with the community, joining in the prayer, the sorrows, the boredoms, the highs, the sins, the reconciliations. It is most powerfully in our common prayer together at Mass that we are most community, most publicly supportive and witnessing.

5. The committment opportunities are to be found all throughout our Parish Booklet which you have received in this packet, especially the list in back. If you need more information, call the name and number listed or the parish office.

6. It is possible, of course, that at this time, in all honesty and integrity, you cannot sign this Covenant. We understand, and will be ready when you can. We are willing to do all we can to support you in coming to a decision. Just keep the form until such a time as you can sign it—and meanwhile call us at any time you want any further discussion or help.

7. Meanwhile, let us all prayer for one another. To be a Christian in the Catholic tradition, to be openly counter-culture is difficult. It is not easy to follow Jesus and his gospel in such an unsettled time. That is precisely why we need each other, precisely why we have to openly support one another, why we have to pledge faithfulness.

of a strict pastor it could be a nasty weapon of discrimination or punishment. This I admit, is all possible, but I still think the pluses outweigh the minuses. First of all, the Covenant is another teaching tool, another concept, vocabulary word (buzz word if you like), like People of God and community, that tries to move people's concept of church away from an exclusively institutional one to a relational one, to a community one. Second, it really is a more personal, one-to-one way to meet new people and discover something of their journey. Talking over and signing the Covenant is a wonderful opportunity to talk and perhaps even (for some) to reenter the church. Third, it offers an opportunity for people to rethink "cheap grace" and presents to them (kindly and sensitively) a badly needed ideal of commitment. It takes membership and partnership seriously, moves them beyond the mere cultural or ethnic label, and lays the groundwork for what we have been talking about: responsibility for ministry and mission.

Finally, the covenant notion tries to make some effort at criteria. I think it was Regis Duffy who said what's wrong with the Catholic church is that it has no criteria for membership.

Consider the following passage from John LeCarrés *The Little Drummer Girl:*

"So what's the bottom line here, Charlie?" Kurtz inquired kindly. "Regarding that whole early period of your life until what we may call the Fall—"

"The age of innocence, Mart?" she suggested helpfully.

"Precisely. Your age of innocence. Define it for me."

"It was hell."

"Want to name some reasons?"

"It was suburbia. Isn't that enough?"

"No, it is not."

"Oh, Mart —you're so—" Her slack-mouthed voice. Her tone of fond despair. Limp gestures with her hand. How could she ever explain? "It's all right for you, you're a Jew, don't you see? You've got these fantastic traditions, the security. Even when you're persecuted, you know who you are, and why."

Kurtz ruefully acknowledged the point.

"But for us—rich English suburban kids from Nowheres-ville—forget it. We had no tradition, no faith, no self-awareness, no nothing."

"But you told me your mother was Catholic."

"Christmas and Easter. Pure hypocrisy. We're the post-Christian era, Mart. Didn't anybody tell you? Faith leaves a vacuum behind era, Mart. Didn't anybody tell you? Faith leaves a vacuum behind when it goes away. We're in it."

Here are people without a faith community, a tradition. Well, we tend to let all this slide until we get hit with bad publicity. At the end of 1988, the press made much of the announcement from the Alan Guttmacher Institute (affiliated with Planned Parenthood) that Catholic women, despite the church's teaching and the pope's warnings, have this country's largest share of abortions, 30 percent more than Protestant women. Pro-abortionists have been quick to seize on the statistic. Bishop McHugh of the Archdiocese of Newark (NJ) was equally quick to point out that many of the women in the survey were nominal Catholics. "We have no way of knowing the commitment or true religiosity of these women, whether they were reached or even *can* be reached by the church." Then Father John Gouldrick, director of the National Conference of Catholic Bishops' Pro-Life Activities, jumps in and adds, "Complicating this profile are different concepts of church membership among different denominations. Catholics who have drifted away from the church often describe themselves as Catholic." Are they or aren't they? You see the problem. You can't have it both ways.

The ambiguity of Catholic identification is also very evident in Vatican II's great and pervasive insistence on community and the consequent communal aspect of worship, the sacraments, and the shared faith life. The sacraments are ideally celebrated communally, for they belong to the community. The R.C.I.A. tells us that prospective converts are to be evangelized no longer one-on-one but by the entire community, and at different times they must take public steps of intent, promise, and progress before the assembled community. Father Philip Murnion, director of the National Pastoral Life Center, holds that the priesthood will be strengthened and made attractive to candidates if the church insists "on clear and demanding criteria for those who will exercise priestly ministry." Yet, ironically, there are no criteria for those to whom this ministry will be directed.

In the context of all of this, is someone still a Catholic who retains only the ethnic label or touches the anonymous (to him or her) faith community only at Christmas and Easter? We hasten to add that it's never a question of the person's personal holiness or how he or she lives out of the corporal and spiritual works of mercy. Such works may be heroic enough to put us to shame. That's not the issue. The issue is whether such a Lone Ranger hero can, every few years, legitimately ride into the churchy corral for communal moments and ride out again and still be considered a member. Is such a Christian Clint Eastwood a community member? A prophet? A long-ago baptized infant with "rights" but no obligations? Or is he or she, in Father Gouldrick's words, "a drifter" with the implication of non-alignment?

It's a vexing question and I don't have the answer. Usually, the fantasy that runs through my mind goes like this. A close-knit family is sitting around the table at Christmas. Suddenly the doorbell rings and the door opens and in bounds Mike Eastwood, who lives six blocks away. "Hi, everybody," he cries and makes himself at home at the table. They greet Mike and as he helps himself to some dinner he looks around and asks about their grandma, "a great lady." There's a short silence and finally someone says "Grandma died last January." "Oh, sorry," says Mike between forkfuls. "Say, how's Mary these days, the light of my life"? More silence until someone says, "Mary got married last March and is living in Cleveland." "Really?" say Mike. "So, how's Joey like school?" Someone answers that Joey was hit by a car last month and is recuperating in the hospital. And so it goes, till Mike wipes his mouth, gets up, and leaves with "By the way, I'm getting married next October. I want you, Bob, to be my best man and I'd like to use your limo, Bob. I want all of you to be there. Take care, see you later."

Well, I grant you this is an overbaked fantasy, but its extremes points up the elements that cause the problem. In no way has Mike been a part of that family community—its highs and lows, its weddings and deaths, its excitements and boredoms, its sins and reconciliations—even though he lives only six blocks away. Is he entitled to break bread with them? Is he entitled to their commitment at his wedding, to their communal ministrations and presence? Is he a friend, a "family" member? He deserves to be treated with prayer and his good deeds deserve to be praised. But are there any communal connections? Does the fact that he once grew up with this family make him communally "viable"? Does he have a right to the family limousine? My heart says yes, for who knows that this last act of kindness may not turn the tide. Yet my head asks, At what point must people assume responsibility for their decisions, their lives? It's a tension. As I said, we don't have the answers here. But we do have a Covenant to at least invite some reflection on what is happening when one applies for membership in a faith community.

In practice, we more than err on the lenient side. We do listen to people's stories and are quite tolerant of shortcomings. For the faithful, the Covenant is a welcome and easy thing to sign. For the lukewarm, it's a point of reflection. For the indifferent, it's a challenge. By and large, reaction has been positive, even though most find this approach novel. Originally, we have used the Covenant exclusively for newcomers as a way of joining the parish. Of late, we have extended the Covenant to parishioners who might have lapsed, again as a talking and discussion point, an invitation, really, to rethink their membership in more faithful terms.

To the extent that we use the Covenant as an invitation to talk and as an opportunity to meet personally with the people, we fulfill the requirements Monsignor Joseph Champlin has sensitively set out for dealing with the marginal Catholic. He offers ten suggestions, or guidelines, in his approach, and although I don't think he pays sufficient attention to both the communal nature of Christianity and the communal identity of the faith-community and its privileged actions, the sacramental celebrations, these suggestions are worth noting:

1. In all requests for sacraments, discuss the situation during personal interviews, never over the telephone. [The Covenant automatically sets this up.]

2. Explain clearly the church's lofty expectations and encourage petitioners to strive for these ideals. [Don't, in other words, play cop; play Christ.]

3. Insist, but with an understanding flexibility, upon attendance at some sort of educational and formational preparation for the sacrament.

4. Involve committed lay persons as teachers and sponsors, models and helpers in these sacramental preparation efforts. [We do this at all levels and it is effective.]

5. Urge regular participation in Sunday Mass, recent recourse to penance, and frequent reception of the Eucharist, but do not mandate these as essential requirements for baptism, marriage, or other similar sacramental encounters. [I agree, but it seems something more ought to be considered for proven marginal Catholics. If, for example, such people in fact have not participated and do not participate in any of the faith community's life, what is happening when, say, they initiate their child into the community-based baptism celebration whose whole meaning and power *are* communal? Is living even a holy life totally apart from the faith community enough to justify communally-orientated sacramental celebrations for those who meet the community only for the moment and depart again? Is there some good-will sign needed here beyond the fact that they asked for the sacraments at all? Does experience count here, namely, a priest who has been in a parish for some

twenty-five years and has consisently witnessed a certain family appearing only at sacramental need times, in spite of consistent and kind invitations?]

6. Encourage parish registration, but do not demand reception or use of church envelopes as a requisite for a sacrament, except in cases of those persons who live outside the parish territory.

7. Treat each request on an individualized basis, helping the parents, the engaged couple, or the petitioner come to decisions, which they alone make, about their own faith and readiness for the sacrament they ask.

8. Facilitate the petitioners' active involvement in the preparation and execution of the liturgy so that the liturgical celebration itself will sustain, strengthen, and deepen the recipient's faith.

9. Never refuse, only delay, celebration of any sacrament. [Good point. Always leave the door open].

10. Strive to imitate Christ, the suffering servant Messiah who was extremely careful not to break the bruised reed or to snuff out the smoldering wick, and who cautioned against pulling up the weeds before the harvest, lest the wheat by uprooted as well. [Surely something to take to heart—although, of course, it's always chancy to quote the scripture selectively. Among his consoling words, Jesus did in fact call some human beings hypocrites, blind guides, whitewashed tombs, serpents, broods of vipers and asked how they could think of escaping hell—pretty reed-bruising stuff! (Matthew, 23:13 ff; Luke 11:37). Furthermore, those who did not believe in him have the devil as their father (John 8:44) and would die in their sins (John 8:24) (pretty wick-snuffing, if you ask me!); and when many of his disciples "left him and stopped going with him," he let them go and simply asked the others, "What about you, do you want to go away too?" (John 6:67)—a weed-pulling, solong, Fellas scenario, it would seem.]

But truly, there's much wisdom in these ten suggestions and having "models, helpers" and teachers plus a sensitive dialogue occasioned by the Covenant can be very helpful in "challenging but not crushing" the marginal Catholic and challenging and affirming the practicing Catholic.[1]

❑ Once a year we have our "Oliver" celebration for all new families. The name comes from the song in the musical "Oliver": "Consider yourself at home, consider yourself one of the family." We send invitations, and included in the invitation is a piece of a puzzle. One of our creative people in charge of the event had a photograph of our parish church blown up, then jig-sawed it into many pieces. A piece is mailed and, of course, part of the Oliver celebration ceremony is for each family to add its piece until the whole "community" is built up—the unity coming from their diversity. At the celebration there are booths around the hall hawking the various parish ministries. There is a skit done by several families. Each person or family is introduced and a brief history given on what brought them to the parish. Then refreshments are served and all receive a gift: always a small green plant, symbol of new life, new growth and, our organic unity.

CHAPTER 9

Identity
and Imagery

The children of the darkness are always smarter than the children of the light. We know that bit of wisdom not only from good authority, but from experience as well. The "children of darkness," in this case, is the corporation. Through various means the corporation spends millions of dollars cultivating—and protecting—its identity and imagery. In 1988, the Philip Morris Corporation bought out Kraft products because they found that just the trade name of Kraft guaranteed sales. In fact, research shows that over the decades the brand names have been a source of steady profit in good times and in bad. The parish could learn from the corporation. Of course, we aren't "in business" in the monetary sense, but surely we're in business in the evangelization sense, in the sense of trying to be an identifiable presence of the Lord in our time and place.

To promote good parish identity and imagery, I would like to offer the following anagram, an outrageously forced one, I admit: T.H.E. P.S.A.L.M.S. (All of the letters rate a ❏ but I won't clutter the text with them here).

T = *Theme*. Each year the parish council meets to come up with a theme for the forthcoming parish year (September to June). The theme is our overall guide and thrust for the year, and we try to weave it throughout our activities. The theme is a kind of goal or reminder, and as such it is a rallying and identity point for us. For example, last year our theme was "Marketplace Spirituality." So this theme appeared as the title of our annual parish booklet; we gave a series of sermons on the topic; we gave a workshop on it and several of our retreats and days of recollection replayed the theme. And it forms the topic of our annual "State of the Parish" address.

❏ The "State of the Parish" address is one that I as pastor give at all the Masses, usually on the third Sunday of September when everyone is back from vacation. It's not a talk about finances at all. It's a combination of where-we've-been, where-we-are, and where-we're-going pep talk. It tells us how great we are, how wonderful the people are, what a good parish we are, and introduces our theme for the year—what we hope to be alert to and think about and work at. The address ends up with a sincere thank you for the past year and a challenge for the coming year.

I've been in the parish since 1973. Here are our themes for each of those years and their progressive moments in our communal lives:

1973   "The Year of Community" (people did not know each other so this theme was clearly saying, "Come, let us get to know each other")

1974   "The Year of Faith" (reflecting the Holy Year)

1975   "The Year of the Spirit" (the first time we had Confirmation in the new church building)

1976   "The Year of Signs" (going over the revised rituals and sacraments.)

1977   "The Year of Spiritual Renewal" (introduction of prayer groups, the Divine Office, and a parish mission)

1978   "The Year of Vision" (looking forward to building our Spiritual Center. More on that later).

1979   "The Year of Celebration" (dedication of Spiritual Center and my silver jubilee).

1980   "The Year of the Parish Family" (reflecting U.S. Bishops' Year of the Family).

1981   "The Year of Affirmation" (affirming the growing number of involved people).

1982   "The Year of Time Remembered" (reviewing our teaching of who and what we are).

1983   "The Year of We Are a People in Christ" (each month of this year we developed, preached on, and taught a special catch up theme of renewal).

1984   "The Year of Preparing the Way of the Lord" (getting ready for the diocese-wide Renew program).

1985   "The Year of Invitation and Response" (Renew is here).

1986   "The Year of Morning Has Broken" (celebrating our Sharing Shed and the beginning of our outdoor Grotto and my four-month sabbatical at Boston College).

1987   "The Year of Expansions" (the Grotto done, a parish center proposed [turned down], and plans for a much needed expansion of the parish offices).

1988   "The Year of Marketplace Spirituality" (responding to Vatican II's universal call to holiness. See Chapter 1).

1989   "The Year of R.C.I.A." (We spent the past year training the facilitators and "practicising" with a few candidates. Now we want to sensitize the whole faith community to the power and meaning of the R.C.I.A.)

The theme, or goal setting, is a small but telling part in our identity and imagery.

H = *History*. Every parish has a story, even a recent one. People, some of whom have moved a great deal, need a sense of roots, a sense of history. Like a family album, the parish should have some means of keeping before the people's eyes a sense of movement, progress, and, above all, those people on whose shoulders we all stand. So we have two approaches.

❑ A Parish History. Years ago, we gathered people to collect material for our history. We're a 105-year-old parish; for 88 years of those years we were a small mission to several mother parishes in the region. We went to the natives and old folk and got their old photographs and remembrances and often tape recorded them. Then we put all the material together and ran a series on our long history in our quarterly publication, *The Mustard Seed*. The series was fascinating and well received. And it served the purpose of giving us a sense of "roots and wings."

❑ A Pictorial Wall. We had one of our able parishioners put up a wall over the cinder block wall of our Spiritual Center. Then we put together both text and photographs from the past to the present, had them professionally mounted, and attached them on the wall to be a permanent pictorial history of our parish for all to see.

E = *Exposure*. This refers to the photographs we have in church. We have permanent photographs hanging around the church showing our communal life from worship to play. On our large bulletin board we have temporary photographs of current events and affairs that change every six or seven weeks. In addition, since we do have many events and take lots of pictures, we gather them into albums that we leave all over the place for people to look through. Furthermore:

❑ Photos. We have taken the best of our many pictures and put them into one large master album, which we have enshrined in the foyer of our Spiritual Center (not far from our pictorial history wall) so that both natives and visitors can look at it. Also,

❑ Videotapes. We have videotapes made of the larger events (such as our variety show, dedication, etc.), which we reproduce and sell. We are now in the process of putting together an hours' composite that will give an overview of our parish life.

P = *Presento*. Here is a subtlety. We make a distinction between presenting and sponsoring. We do this to prevent unseemly competition among the organizations, and to teach a more corporate sense of parish. Translated, this means that although a particular organization may be the main (and perhaps only) sponsor of an event, it is always the parish that presents it. So, for example, "St. Mary's presents a Valentine Dance, sponsored by the Martha/Mary Guild [your Rosary-Altar] and the Men's Guild [your Holy Name]." "St. Mary's presents Adult Education, a Christmas trip, etc." sponsored by this or that organization or group.

This emphasis keeps the corporate parish in the forefront and cements the parish identity and imagery.

S = *Solo*. This may sound like a contradiction, but "Solo" refers to the reality of the mystique of the pastor, which means that I sign all public letters and flyers. I am seen as the corporate person (alas, a trade name), and even though an affair presented by the parish and sponsored by an organization, my name goes on the bottom of the announcement. It's like Lee Iacocca or Betty Crocker. It's trading on the corporate rallying persona, and so it helps the identity.

A = *Argot*. This refers to the written word, which, in turn, means our quarterly publication mentioned above, posters, flyers, and our annual parish booklet. Not least of all, it also means easy communication. Having about a thousand names to send to, we have an antiquated old addressograph that punches out names on envelopes, a wonderful group of people every day who sort, stuff, and mail, and our mailing permit. Within a day or two we can get a parish-wide mailing out. (Yes, we could go modern via computer and automatic stamping and sorting, but replace all those people? Never.)

❑ College Newsletter. About half dozen times a year we

send material to all our college kids. For several weeks in the Fall we have a notice in the bulletin asking for their college addresses. We'll drop anything into the newsletter: the parish bulletin, articles, Thanksgiving greetings, etc. The last two times, I recall, we sent some very fine articles on Fundamentalism because we knew that our kids would sooner or later be hit with attractive proselytizers. We also sent a great article on college and value and self worth that was well received. But we're not out to preach or teach. The main thrust is a parish hello, mail from home.

❑ Project Post. This is something like Telecare, except it's by mail. We take the updated parish list and divide it among the organizations. Members who wind up with 10 or 15 names will drop the people a line twice a year: just "how are you" and "we think of you, are grateful for you," etc. And it's from a fellow parish member. It's a small, but nice thing to do.

L = *Logo*. Long ago we adopted a logo for our parish and I recommend it to all. Ours is a Dove, a sign of (we hope) a Spirit-filled and Spirit-led community. We put it on our stationery, flyers, parish booklet, notices—everywhere. People identify the parish with it, as much as you identify brand name products with certain logos. So find a logo that you think expresses who you are and then market it as your own. It will help your imagery and identity.

M = *Motto*. In the same way, get yourself a motto. Ours is "A Christian Community in the Roman Catholic Tradition" and it appears on all of our official materials. We're a community in that we identify with all of humanity. Within that common humanity, we believe in the Lordship of Jesus Christ. Within those communities that do believe in the Lordship of Christ, we stand in the Roman Catholic tradition of that belief and expression.

S = *Servo*. I'll mention our coordinator of volunteers in another chapter, but here I want to emphasize one aspect of accessibility that I mentioned earlier in regard to service:

❑ The Common Office. Among the offices you'll see in the parish with its various titles on the door, you'll find one marked "Common Office." In it there is a desk and a phone. The purpose of this office, of course, is to be of benefit to all the volunteers and various other helpers that we have. You can't ask people to do something and not provide them with the necessary tools. Often, such volunteers need a desk and access to a phone to do their jobs. The public availability of our common office at any hour of the day or night grants them this right and symbolically says we take their service seriously.

We also express our regard for service by each year having a dedication in our annual Parish Booklet. After the theme, the dedication is spelled out. Over the years, we have dedicated those booklets to our former pastor, the behind-the-scenes people, our senior parishioners, the deceased, our volunteers, our first woman associate pastor, our oldest parishioner (102 years old), our DREs, etc. In short, those who do service.

❑ A "Volunteer Record" is issued. This was inspired by the United States bishops' pastoral on women, noting the financial worth of both male and female volunteer service and an appreciation for the worth of their service. The Volunteer Record (with our Logo on it, of course) is issued for each separate task or once a year at the end of an ongoing or enduring task, for example, CCD teacher, cantor, etc. Here is the text:

> Before you begin your service, we ask that you take this sheet and, after the task is done, fill it out, and return to this office.
>
> The purpose of this record is not to compete with another, not to accumulate numbers, not to reduce your service to mathematics. Rather, this record is our means of giving you

> RECOGNITION
>
> It means that:
> 1. We are aware of what you're doing, deeply admire and appreciate it, and never take it for granted.
> 2. We know that in monetary value your work and time would be considerable, and likely beyond our ability to

pay. We are sensitive to that. And:

3. We want to have this record go with you if you ever move away so that others may know of your contribution to this parish community.

> Sincerely and gratefully,
> Fr. Bausch and St. Mary's Parish

Then there is a bottom tear-off, listing the volunteer's name, date, project, the hours invested, and space for any comments and suggestions.

So there you have it: T (theme), H (history), E (exposure), P (presento), S (solo), A (argot), L (logo), M (motto), and S (servo), a clumsy assist toward a very unclumsy reality: the imagery and identity of your parish.

The complete Parish Census Form is presented as an appendix to this book, since it is the most asked-for item. We designed this several years ago. It's not especially scientific, but we found it useful and it helped us make many changes.

As a kind of footnote to this chapter, if I were pressed to give a long-range process and goal for the parish, I would suggest to new pastors or pastoral administrators that they might entertain the following agenda—the time frames being more but not less:

First three years—Getting to know the territory and teaching in any way you can what the faith and a faith community are all about (homilies, lectures, goal setting, etc.). All the while, of course, encouraging shared and collaborative ministries that should flow from the teaching.

Two years—Introduce and work such programs as RENEW in the parish. (A year to prepare, a year to get it going).

Two years—Introduce the R.C.I.A., for now, after five years of teaching and doing, there should be developing a sense of community to make it work.

Two to three years—Create small faith communities or base communities in the parish. The RENEW groups will have seeded the idea and will have gotten people used to them.

So here you have a long-range, almost ten-year program or ongoing goal, a sense of rhythm, of going somewhere as this faith community. I do think that the end of the process would be small faith communities and I would recommend the work of Father Arthur Baranowski from Michigan. (He's put it in print and on video: "Creating Small Faith Communities," *St. Anthony Messenger Press.*)

CHAPTER 10

Three
That Count

Before we discuss the philosophy of staff, there are three staff members that, ideally, every parish ought to have. The first is a Coordinator of Volunteers. We have already alluded to the fact that if there are to be volunteers, then surely you must give them the tools to work with. There is nothing more frustrating (and demeaning) than to ask a volunteer to take on some project and then walk away or leave them to their own resources. Because we are aware of this, we have a retired gentleman who draws a salary and acts as the coordinator of volunteers. This is in addition to the accessibility of the common office mentioned in the last chapter.

Volunteers, as we all know, need certain basics: stamps, envelopes, addresses, and so on. So we give each of our volunteers this little notice. Since our coordinator of Volunteers is named Joe we have some fun with the notice, which goes like this:

❑ Attention All Volunteers

Your Scripture Passage from now on is Genesis 41:55. Of course, you all know that's the passage where the Pharaoh says to all who come to him for help, "Go to Joseph." So it is with you. From now on, if you need stamps, envelopes, phones, addresses, paper, things typed or copies run off—whatever you need—"Go to Joseph!"

"Joseph" being in this case, Joe George, who is in charge of volunteers and has his office in the Spiritual Center. He's there daily from 10:00 A.M. to 2:00 P.M.

Be holy. Do not go to the parish office for your needs, but to the Spiritual Center and so fulfill the Scriptures: Genesis 41:55.

So Joe has all the materials listed in his office, plus a typewriter and copier and phone. The volunteers just place an order with him and he gives them the supplies or runs off the material they need. There's a sense of dignity and justice to the whole setup.

The second staff member is an on-the-premises counselor. The origin of this goes back about ten years. A man from another parish wanted to become a permanent married deacon and his own pastor would not sponsor him. I did—but with the condition that he attach himself also to some ministry. I was afraid that if my successor did not want deacons he'd wind up like some overgrown altar boy sitting in the pews. I was also not quite sure myself of the identity of the deacon, with lay people more and more baptizing, witnessing marriages, visiting the sick, doing works of charity, lectoring, bringing Communion and pastoring. I also noted that some dioceses had put a hold on the diaconate program. Anyway, I asked him what he might be interested in and he said he wasn't sure but he was happily married and would like others to be so. So we reached an agreement. The parish would finance his education at Iona College where he would get his degree in counseling, and in turn he would give the parish free time. So for three years he went to Iona and after that he gave many evenings a week and Saturdays to the parish. Eventually we hired him full time. He's an excellent counselor. He does all of our premarriage work (we have a stricter requirement than the preCana and Marriage Encounter—and the diocese itself for that matter.) Ralph will give the engaged couples many, many hours. He now also does family counseling and all kinds of other counseling and is currently getting his state certificate from Seton Hall University.

For me personally, being all alone, as well as for the parish at large, it's a boon to have a full-time counselor on the premesis. I could not handle all of the counseling needs nor would I be capable of it. The presence and support of a counselor on the parish proclaims our values of providing help. His being also a deacon gives a nice religious dimension to the help that is given.

The third "necessary" staff person is a parish spiritual director. The origin of this also goes back about ten years. I felt that, again, since I was all alone, there should be some full-time person to do justice to the spiritual needs of the people in ways that I could not. I was also anxious to bridge the gap between the "mountain" and the "plain," between the desert and the city. In short, I wanted it known that people don't always have to go to remote retreat houses or some monastery to find spiritual direction. I wanted that "marketplace" accessibility too. I wanted the position itself to say something about the intent and spiritual seriousness of the faith community. So, at the time, the parish once more sent our associate, Sister Joan, to Creighton University to get her degree in spiritual direction. She did very well—and we were fortunate to have fine ongoing supervision for her from a spiritual center nearby.

When she left a few years ago, we quickly interviewed others and got another full-time parish spiritual director. She gives talks on spiritual direction, "marketplace" retreats on the property and in the homes for busy people, days of recollection and weekend days of recollection, a course on the spiritual readings of the masters of the spiritual life, directed prayer weekends, midlife workshops (the parish sent her away and funded her certification) and has currently about 61 directees. Our current spiritual director is a nun, but we have under training a married woman, mother of two (she'll be fully certified in another year) and are priming a layman also to become a spiritual director. We know that we can eventually use three full-time directors—so much has this caught on and so much has their very presence and work enhanced the parish.

So that's my belief: Every parish (presuming you can afford it) should have these three staff members—or at least have them shared among several parishes—a coordinator of volunteers, a counselor, and a spiritual director. These three are not only a reality in our parish, they are a symbol of the parish's values and priorities. (We have someone in charge of social concerns but she is not paid staff. More on "helping hands" later).

As for the staff itself, I have my own philosophy and practice. The staff understands its role strictly as *servant* to the community. This may sound banal, but it's really important. What it means is that our staff does not make policies and does not plan and does not decide on programs. Members of the staff, of course, like any other parishioners, may have input on all the three, but they are not the final word or the direct initiators. If they have a great idea, they too must pass it through the regular process. In our parish that process is this: planning and programs (done after Easter for the coming parish year) are done by an independent ad hoc committee and passed through the parish council. The significance of this is that people do not have to "walk around" the staff, get the staff's permission or feel that they have to answer to the staff as they would if the staff were the chief architects of everything. The staff is there for *their* needs, not the other way around. The staff should not be the collective old stereotyped housekeeper that simultaneously runs the parish and protects the pastor. The staff facilitates the parish's needs, and serves those needs.

It does not make the needs for people to serve. That attitude and policy, I think, are critical for parish health and freedom.

I might add, by the way, as I did in a previous book, that if at all possible, I would never let the staff have its offices in the rectory. The priest's (or pastor's, lay, religious, or cleric) private life and work should be just that, private, and people should not be subject to the gauntlet of peering eyes and knowing nods when they come to visit the priest either socially or professionally.

❏ An Idea: F.O.C.U.S. This stands for "Faith Occasions Community Under the Spirit"—another forced anagram, but one that gets the message across. The program was to invite (strongly and urgently) all of the staff and all of the heads of the many ministries to a five-part preparatory series. This one year we "cancelled" the month of September and devoted that month to catch-up and refreshment for the staff and ministers. Here's the topic list (with the old dates):

September 15—Dr. Jerome Leary [a clinical psychologist] on "Effective Leadership"

September 21—Fr. Jim O'Brien [superior spiritual director and guide] on "Growing in Relationship with God"

September 22—Dr. Jerome Leary on "Groups and Groups" [group dynamics]

September 26—Sister Pat and Fr. Jay on "The Myers Briggs and Me"

September 29—Sr. Maureen Conroy [another superior spiritual guide] on "Prayer and Discernment"

October 5—Mass followed by a banquet at a fine restaurant.

You can see from the topics that we were refreshed in our vision. Through urging and invitation we had almost 100 percent of our 60 some people present for all sessions. It was a great way to begin the year. Sometimes every few years you have to "shut down" the calendar for just such a renewal. I might add that like most places, we do take time apart during the year with the immediate staff. We have an overnight at a mountain cabin, a day away, and an annual "mystery" ride. We also have:

❑ The "Christmas in January" Thank You Party. We invite all those volunteers who did something in the past year (about 300 of them) to a stand up cocktail party at the end of January: our Christmas in January thank you. We give them a token gift, have a band there, and provide catered food.

There is one final, if subtle, word I would like to share on the topic of staff. It has to do with spirituality; that is, the spirituality of the one who hires. We all have our deficiencies, and none of us likes to have them underscored or highlighted by others' gifts. And so, for self-protection, we who do the hiring of staff consciously or unconsciously place some mental escape clauses in our private contracts or agendas which allow us to "keep in their place" or cause to eventually leave those who show us up or put us in the shadow. They have talent. People are attracted to them and their (successful) programs. They are preferred. Understandably, no official leader is easily going to shout hoorah over that. The only thing that helps us to overcome this tension is a genuine attempt to see the larger picture, to look to the overall "enterprise."

That enterprise comes back to our first "C" in Chapter 5: Concept. What are you in the business for except to promote the kingdom of God—and in the best possible way with the best possible people? What's the job of the parish except to be a living faith community centered around the Lordship of Jesus who had some gentle but pointed words for his disciples who were arguing over who was the greatest and suggested that we become as little children. Whatever dynamic is at work, whatever past insecurities, it is our prayer life, our constant rededication to the larger picture, our John the Baptist "he-must-increase-I-must-decrease" posture that will make us determined to assemble the best staff we can. That we might get somewhat overshadowed is part of the "kenosis," or emptying out, that our Leader underwent, a sharing in his passion and mission. That is why I said that ultimately, when you think about it, the choice of a staff is a matter of spirituality and is a challenge to growth.

CHAPTER 11

Helping Hand

Most parishes have many direct and creative ways to help people not only in their everyday lives but also in emergencies. That help ranges from counseling and referrals to sophisticated food and clothing programs. What I want to list here—in no particular order—are other programs that might be new for some.

❑ The Wailing Wall. This any parish can do. It takes little space and has such an appeal that the day we completed it it was abundantly used. The Wailing Wall is simply some space in your church, some angle or blank wall, that you cover with cork or similar material. Our Wailing Wall is made up of cork cleverly cut out to simulate brick. Then this material is set off by a wide wooden frame. In the middle of this wall is a framed notice that explains it all, including a nice twist:

What you see here is an idea inspired by the Wailing Wall in Jerusalem (properly called the Western Wall, that is, the western wall of the old Temple.

Here, generations of people have prayed and cried out their needs before God. Indeed, to this day, little pieces of paper with prayers and petitions are rolled up and inserted in the broken mortar between the bricks of the wall.

Our own Wailing Wall serves the same purpose. It is here in order that (1) you might tack your needs and prayers and petitions to it so that all who pause may see, be moved, and prayer, or (2) you might take the petition off the wall and keep it for a week and pray for the unknown writer whose heart is broken. Then you might initial it and put it back again so that the person who put it there originally may know that he or she is not alone; that someone gave comfort, sympathy, and concern.

In any case, the Wailing Wall stands as a small shrine, a special place in our church where we stand with deep devotion and piety and raise our hearts and minds to God with longing, tears, and confidence.

Feel free, then, to tack on your needs and look over others' needs. Most of all, stand there with a reverence and quiet that deep sympathy and charity always demand of us all.

There are pins and paper in the corner for people to use. The Wailing Wall is an impressive sight. It's still more impressive to read the heart-rending needs, and yet heartening to see the initialed papers returned there, too. This is a simple, effective project.

❏ In our vestibule on the book rack are "Caring Cards." The text is as follows:

St. Mary's Parish Caring Card
Colts Neck, NJ

If you know of a parishioner who is ill or a shut-in or who needs some help, please fill in this card and drop it into collection basket or at the parish office or mail it in.

Request for_____
(Name and address)
Phone_____
Sick or elderly ❑ at home ❑ in hospital ❑ which hospital?
❑ Would like Communion ❑ Needs Sacrament of the Sick
❑ Needs assistance in getting to church ❑ Would just like a visit
❑ Include in Prayers of the Faithful ❑ other (use reverse of card)
Your name and phone number_____
Thank you!

❑ Frozen Meals. This is easy and effective and requires little space except a freezer or two (bought or donated). Twice a year we publicize in the bulletin and on posters the need for frozen meals for the sick and shut-ins. On the weekend set aside, we place representative containers (we supply them) on the altar (with the rest in the parish hall behind the church for easy pick up) and bless them before dismissal:

> Loving father, we ask your blessing (+) on these food containers. Be gracious to those who prepare the food and those who eat it and are nourished. Let us be mindful of your constant care and mercy, and bring us all to your eternal banquet. Amen.

Then the people are reminded to pick up the containers in the hall, fill them with whatever meals they're making and return them to the hall next week or during the week where the Samaritans (our help organizations) will place them in the freezers.

❑ Tree of Love. This, I gather, is rather common. We erect a live Christmas tree in the foyer of our spiritual center and on it are paper ornaments listing the actual needs of adults and children. People are asked to "undecorate" the tree by taking off the paper ornament with its request, filling that request, and then bringing back the present and placing it under the tree—with the ornament attached so we know what's inside, for example, a sweater, medium-sized, for an adult woman.

❏ New Year's Insert. This is a kindly insert for your bulletin at the start of a new year. On top of the page is the title "Pilgrimage of Faith: The Beginning and the End," and the wording underneath goes like this:

We offer you the names of those who, during the past year, have either begun or completed their pilgrimage of faith on earth at St. Mary's parish. Please remember them all in your prayers as we begin this New Year of grace.

New Christians (in order of appearance)	Died in the Lord (in order of their death)

Then, of course, gleaned from the records, you list the names of the past year's baptized and deceased under the proper column.

❏ Paint the Windows. Most places have some clear windows on the buildings as we do in our parish hall. So (as do some department stores) for Advent we invite families or friends or kids to paint these windows with Christmas or advent themes. We have someone in charge to provide the (washable) paint and we give out an outline of the window dimensions and segments (so that people can do a whole window or only part of it). It's an outlet for talent, gives the place a holiday look, and displays religious themes that public schools and other buildings can't.

❏ Open House. Several times we've had an open house for the public. We give them a little map (as college campuses do), have guides to show them around the church, the parish house, spiritual center, and Sharing Shed. We have displays of liturgical items in church, such as vestments, vessels, etc., photographs, and a slide show. There are also people on hand who are equipped to explain our way of life and answer any questions. Refreshments are served, of course. The open house is held, rain or shine, from 2:00 to 6:00 on a Sunday afternoon.

❏ Funeral Pennant. We have a flag pole, so every time we have a death in the parish and a funeral we raise the pennant—a simple, plain white affair—under the American flag so that people driving by can see it, know what it means, and offer a prayer for the deceased and the family. If you don't have a flag pole, you could hang the pennent from a prominant window or the like.

❑ Caregivers. This is rather new to us, but we have sensed a need due to the simple arithmetic of the elderly—by the year 2030, according to the Census Bureau, one fifth of all Americans will be 65 or over. But, of course, even now, adult children and nursing home and hospice workers and volunteers are giving a lot of care and experiencing a lot of stress. So we're trying to meet this need and our advertising flyer went like this:

To All Caregivers...

Having a family member who is sick or elderly and who can no longer care for himself or herself is possibly one of the most difficult adjustment in family relationships that we will ever make. Objectivity can be completely lost because of our concern for this person whom we have always loved. It's a very hard situation.

We at St. Mary's recognize the difficulties involved for you as caregiver—the anxiety, the stress, the frustration, perhaps even the anger with the person or guilt over difficult decisions you have to face with your loved one who now requires so much of your time and concern.

To respond to this dilemma we are having an initial meeting on Thursday evening, January 19th at 8:00 P.M. in the Spiritual Center. The purpose? To discuss mutual problems, needs, resources and strategies for support and coping.

So we invite all Caregivers to come. It will be a worthwhile evening.

If you're interested, fill out the form below and return to Peggy DePol, 8 Amsterdam Ct., Colts Neck, NJ 07722 or call after 6:00 P.M. 946-4022.

❑ Garden for the Poor. Behind our parish house (rectory)

we have prepared a garden for the poor. Such a garden can be anywhere, or part of several people's own vegetable gardens. We have volunteers who prepare the ground, plant the vegetables, weed and harvest and then take the vegetables to the Mercy Sisters who work in a very depressed area not far from us. They in turn provide fresh vegetables to the elderly poor who are on fixed incomes.

❑ Martin House Helpers. Teens, young adults, and men and women go the diocesan inner-city project once a month to help rebuild houses, bought by the diocese with the poor. No skills are needed, but theys are useful in helping these people in the inner city reclaim their dignity.

❑ The Lazarus Ministry. This has been noted in my other books. It's a wonderful and beautiful ministry. When a call comes in that someone has died, the head of the Lazarus ministry is notified and he or she, with one or two others, immediately visits the home of the bereaved to give comfort and prepare the liturgy. They bring the fine booklet we have put together so the people can pick out the readings, choose readers and offertory bearers if they wish (including the bearing of any personal symbol of the deceased). The family can choose to have a one-night wake in the parish church. If they choose the church wake, then the Lazarus ministry people meet the body at the church when it arrives, provide hospitality in the hall attached to the church, provide coffee and cookies and presence for visitors, and conduct the wake service. The body stays in church overnight and then we have the Mass of Christian Burial at the customary daily 9:00 A.M. Mass. We seldom have a separate Mass for burial. There are many advantages to this. The usual morning people—about 40 to 60 daily—are there to provide tone and direction, and voices for singing. (We have cantoring, lectoring and homilies daily anyway) and to form a representative community. The Lazarus ministry will follow up with visits and grieving and also offer them an invitation, when they're ready, to our Bereavement Group, which meets monthly on Sundays. This ministry has been one of our most powerful, effective, inspirational ministries to Catholics and non-Catholics alike. Often people who have been helped by one bereavement group later came back to work in this ministry. In this way, grieving parishioners are helped by other parishioners who have suffered a similar loss: for example, a parent who has lost a child, a young spouse who has lost his or her spouse, or a parent of a child who has commited suicide.

❑ When the body is brought into church (when it is not waked there) we always have the coffin brought all the way inside toward the front (near the front pews) where it rests before the baptismal font. This is to allow everyone on the outside to come inside so that they can see and hear the opening ceremonies and prayers. It's no use having half of the assembly outside or in the vestibule trying to hear your loud voice "saying or doing something in there." By the way, having the coffin rest against the baptismal font, which is in the front center aisle, gives a marvelous opportunity to make St. Paul's opening words appropriate ("being baptized into Jesus' death") and the pall a real symbol of baptismal fidelity (on God's part).

❑ Lazarus Follow Up. We have a sheet for one of the Lazarus members which reminds them to follow up after the funeral and help with the bereavement time by means of cards and personal visits and phone calls. The sheet, presented here, is one of those things you hang on the refrigerator door as a reminder.

Personal assignment for _____

Name of Deceased_____

Date of death _____

Nearest kin _____

Address _____

Phone _____

Schedule

I. Cards

First month, date sent _____

Second month, date sent _____

Fourth month, date sent _____

Sixth month, date sent _____

II. Personal Visit or Phone Call
First month, date ————————————————————
Third month, date————————————————————
Fifth month, date ————————————————————

III. The Parish Anniversary Card
Sent. O.K.

❑ A Directory for Help. One section of our parish booklet has a small directory where people can go for qualified help and programs ranging from Marriage Encounter, Cursillo, Birthright, and Exceptional Children, to alcoholic and drug recovery units, Compassionate Friends (parents who have lost children), adoptive parents' organizations and the Women's Survival Center.

Here are some more of our parish's "helping hands":

❑ AIDS hotline

❑ Advocate for the Handicapped. Someone who sees that we're sensitive to the needs and access of the handicapped.

❑ Food Collection. The last Sunday of every month is our Food collection Sunday when people bring food and paper goods and lay them in front of the altar.

❑ Nullities. Many years ago I helped a man and woman get two annulments each and finally get their marriage blessed. Faithful and grateful, they now help those seeking annulments, telling them what documents they need, giving them the diocesan forms, and helping them fill them out and what to put in them. They've become quite expert and can naturally empathize with the people in their situation. Whenever anyone calls for an annulment, it's nice just to be able to refer them to this couple.

❑ Twinning. In the back of our church is a native banner from Chile, portraying our two churches and hands from each breaking bread. It's colorful and it's a reminder that we have a twin parish in Chile that we support by our money and prayers. We exchange photographs and people as well.

❑ Appalachia Week. Members of the parish, adults and youth, along with other parishes and schools, give one week of the year to go and work in the Appalachia area.

❑ "Fired, Retired, Searching." One of the more painful realities today is that people, especially those who have such identity and self-evaluation and worth tied into their employment, are fired. It makes no difference if you're an office worker or president of the company. Losing one's job cuts across the board. It's a difficult time for those fired, and often, too, for those retired. So once a year or every two years we have an evening's seminar precisely with the title above. We gather three kinds of facilitators: (1) those who in fact have lost their jobs and can share a common personal story about their self-esteem, tensions in the family, social shame, etc.; (2) experts from a nearby community college as well as from the parish who assist with the practical, such as resumes, job hunting, interviews, age discrimination, etc.; and (3) myself or the deacon or anyone who can help discern the spiritual possibilities, reassessments, and opportunities for growth in this very difficult time. It is a good evening that boosts morale and helps build a support group.

❑ The Presbyters. This is a group of retired men that have monthly luncheon meetings and form an able and talented cadre of fix-it help and other assistance around the parish. Their title gives them standing in the parish, and the Presbyters' activities keep them out of their wives' hair.

❑ Finally, among the "helping hands" reach outs, this might be a sensitive one that not everyone might agree with. But try it out. I'll reproduce the exact proposal as I gave it to the Parish Council and others (who all gave their approval).

A proposal...
Those who are single (statistically, the unmarried are society's fastest growing segment) by choice or circumstance, especially the widowed and divorced, often have a deep sense of being cut off from the community. They frequently feel alienated, out of step.

The parish faith community can do something. It can, as we do here, provide a forum for their meeting and healing and our "Singles' Journey" group is doing a marvelous job. But perhaps something more is needed, something that is a more profound symbol from the community. So I propose this for your consideration and comment.

Let the Single Person serve as a temporary (say, for three to six months) eucharistic minister, lector, or usher in our parish community.

Rationale
1. We are considering here all singles who gravitate to St. Mary's, many of whom are outside the parish boundaries and are not official parishioners.
2. The liturgy is our most public gathering and statement of who and what we are.
3. Those who are single, especially the divorced, the widowed, and the gay, are hurting, feeling cut off from the larger community, particularly from the church.
4. They need a public symbol that they belong, are wanted; that our faith community has room for them and indeed is in need of them.
5. A brief term as eucharistic minister, lector, or usher is simply a community gesture of acceptance, an embrace of healing. (Of course, parishioners among them can fill regular terms.)
6. There would, of course, be criteria:

A. They must be Catholic.
B. They must be reconciled; that is, they have come back (or are in the process of returning) to the church through fellowship, Sunday worship, and a sincere desire to journey in faith (presuming they ever left).
C. They must be striving to live a life in accordance with Christ and his church.
D. We would be careful to explain the program to them in terms of our outreach and concern, so they would understand both the limits and the expansiveness of what we're

trying to do. It is hoped our outreach would also encourage them to be part of their own parish communities and become active if they are not already.

The measure of a parish's commitment to the gospel is found, I believe, in how it treats the marginal, the different. A parish that does not permit the separated, the divorced, the homosexual, the single, and the handicapped, to participate fully gives off a message foreign to Jesus who specialized in the marginal. Here's one woman's response to this proposal: "Father, this is a very caring gesture offered to us on our 'journey.' St. Mary's has given so much to me. If it wasn't for what I have gotten from this community, I wouldn't be as far along in my healing from my separation and divorce. I would be happy to serve a term as a eucharistic minister or lector."

We should tack on here, not as an afterthought, but as an essential part of what we're considering, the young adults. Fact: in the United States 68 million men and women (or 41 percent of the population) are young adults between the ages of 18 and 34. This comes to about 15 million young adult Catholics. About half of them are alienated or inactive. Sociologist Dean Hoge found that about 45 percent of church dropouts are twenty-two years of age or younger, about 24 percent return at or before the age of twenty-five, and 53 percent return at or before the age of thirty. Such "in and out" activity urges us to put as much effort and money into this group as we do into teenagers. Perhaps a Young Adult Ministry is also needed (ours is called "Polaris" after the guiding star). Perhaps we can begin by simply asking: Who are these young adults and what are their needs? What are their pressures?

I've noted that single young adult women especially talk of the pressures of dating. Since so many people seem to expect sex on a date, a single person who wants to keep to a moral code has a pretty poor social life. One young man in his late twenties summarizes a familiar theme: "The main satisfactions of being single are (1) being free, (2) having less responsibility, (3) having more time to yourself. The main problems are making quality friendships that last and meeting the right person so you can eventually get married."[1] Loneliness is a problem. The successful woman finds she threatens the male. Although many people, perhaps most, look forward to marriage, some prefer the single life. To this extent they would like their choice to be seen as a positive vocation rather than a state of default. However we understand these huge numbers of singles—never married, divorced, widowed—they, too, are our family.

Many parishes of every stripe and level have "helping hands" programs that leave us all in admiration and awe, and confirm our faith. Those listed in this chapter are just some of the more offbeat ones that fire the imagination, move the heart and remind us of what we're all about.

CHAPTER 12

Family Life

Under the rubric of family life the parish, like so many others, has many opportunities for families to get together, to grow, and to be affirmed. Family life was and remains one of the top concerns of Americans. In that huge survey of active listening years ago sponsored by the United States bishops, the top six distilled priorities were (1) spirituality, (2) marriage and family, (3) the changing role and status of women in society and church, (4) the world of work (marketplace spirituality), (5) ministry and mission, and (6) community.

For many people, these are real flesh and blood concerns. Consider, for example, the woman who wrote the following letter. She began by discussing someone whose religious agenda seemed rather trivial. In contrast, she continues:

The world I deal with ...has tough problems demanding solutions: crime, poverty, drug addiction, child abuse, unemployment, abortion, euthanasia, the homeless, AIDS. I'm concerned every time my teenage sons walk out the door, whether or not someone will try to sell them cocaine. I worry that they'll wind up in an auto accident....I'm much more concerned about all the Catholics who have left us in the past 20 years or so to join other churches. I'm more concerned about the bitterness I sense in letters from persons who condemn anyone whose view of how to live Christianity differs from their own...I'm concerned about Catholics who make $50,000 a year and give $2 a week to their parish, the same as they gave when they were earning $150 a week in 1975. I'm concerned with the gratuitous sex on prime-time television that puts demands on me as a parent I cannot hope to meet...I'm concerned that my kids have been so saturated in sex—you can't escape it for a moment in this media-conscious society we live in—that they have lost all sense of its mystery, magic, and beauty as God's gift to us. I'm concerned for the folks who are worried that a lifetime of savings won't pay for decent medical care when they retire if serious illness should strike. I'm concerned that there has been a general decline of civility in this country, from the surly store clerk who takes my money to the way in which children address their elders with no discernible sign of respect.[1]

These are the concerns of the everyday people of faith and decency, and such concerns present a formidable challenge to the parish faith community. The challenge is formidable for the simple reason that the "systems" (as Jurgen Habermaus terms them) are so powerful. In other words, our economic and administrative systems have become ends in themselves and monopolize the communication systems, forcing us to homogenize our values. Such systems "colonize" everything else. The result is that we feel helpless. As with the mother above, so much is beyond our control. As Robert Bellah puts it:

> Much in the way our society is organized makes us think the pressures we feel are beyond our capacity to resist. Competition is a powerful force and survival a powerful motive. Dare we turn down a monetary advancement, given the high cost of college education for our children and the uncertainty of retirement plans, just because our husband or wife and children would be better off in the place where we presently live? And how can we control what our children are doing? Do we have the authority? Can we set guidelines on the television they watch, or, perish forbid, the music they listen to? And how do we know what they are up to anyway? Powerful outside pressure fragment and atomize the family so that each member goes his or her own way and the home is only a temporary stopping point between lives that are basically unconnected.[2]

Any family life programs must keep these concerns in the background. Beyond the usual programs most parishes have, here are a few suggestions:

❑ Family Sacraments. Keep in mind the last of the three Cs we dealt with in Chapter 6: Cult. By this I mean that it is critical to revive what we might call "family sacraments." The most central is, of course, the family meal. At least several times a week, it should be a house rule that the members eat together. Then there are those recreational and holiday rituals that are so important. There are wonderful little books on various family blessings and books like Sandra DeGidio's *Enriching Faith through Family Celebrations* (Twenty-Third Publications). The parish could note such books in the bulletin and make them available.

❑ The Family Education Program. Most of our families send their children to religious education classes, but we have 30 of them who prefer the Family Ed. program. This meets one Sunday morning a month for two hours. The program has two families develop each month's theme within the preplanned yearly overall theme. The adults and bigger children attend one session while the smaller children are broken down into various age-group classes. A guest speaker takes the first group and the teachers take the second. (Babysitting is provided for the infants and toddlers.) During the second hour all come together to do common projects on the day's lesson, have a mutual celebration, and then end with refreshments. I haven't done justice to the camaraderie, the learning, the closeness of the families. The program is sprinkled with outings, pot luck suppers, square dancing, and retreats.

❑ The Singles' Journey. This has really taken off. This is a group of singles 35 and over who meet every Sunday after the 10:30 Mass. They are the never married, separated, divorced, and widowed of the parish. Initially, there was some fear that the agenda of the widowed and the divorced would be too conflicting, but this has not materialized. For some reason this group has caught fire and new people are added every week by word of mouth. It's self-run and the word I most often hear associated with the group is "healing." One of their number wrote a lovely little descriptive statement, which I pass along in case you ever want to start a similar group.

A Single Journey—Singles over 35
Every Sunday at 11:30, friends gather together here at St. Mary's for an hour or so of companionship, caring, and sharing. We are men and women who came as strangers and are now friends; we are separated, divorced, widowed, or never-married, but find a strong common bond in our struggle to lead a committed Christian life as single persons. Our stories are unique and our paths are diverse, but we share as a common goal the desire to heal, to grow, and to seek new directions in our lives. We understand that for each of us there is a time to speak and a time to listen, and we ask only that all respect the confidentiality of whatever is shared here.

Our purpose is our prayer....

Let us look objectively at the past—to learn from it, never to dwell on it. In each of our histories, let us know which things are to be shared and which should be kept apart.

Let us look kindly at the present. May we be gentle with ourselves and each other for we are at different stages in our journey. We offer fellowship and support, never advice or judgment.

Let us look hopefully at the future! May we see the wonderful possibilities that are open to us as single travelers and may we share both joy and sorrow, laughter and tears as we grow together.

Above all, let us be open to the wisdom in each others' words. May we learn to listen more than we speak; to give more than we gain.

We are here to be here for each other!

The parish must be sensitive to the many singles, especially in its subconscious statements and attitudes. Social affairs tickets, for example, should never be priced for couples. $10 a ticket is pastorally preferable to $20 a couple. If you have Mother's Day or Father's Day sermons, you should stretch the concept to include all those who have parented us in any way: teachers, neighbors, friends, married, or single. The language of homilies should always reflect all levels, not just a word to parents or moms and dads or husbands and wives. Singles should be included in the word "family" so that they are welcomed to the Family Education program, to serve on committees, and are a part of our Saturday night dinners (I invite two couples to the parish house for dinner every Saturday night).

❑ Family High Mass Servers. On the first Sunday of every month at the 12 noon Mass we have a high Mass: traditional choir in robes, all sung parts, the Asperges, incense. On that Sunday we ask a whole family to serve the Mass. It's a one-shot deal for them. Someone rehearses them, and they decide who among them will carry the candles, the holy water, incense, etc.

❑ Monthly Birthday Celebrations. Once a month at a daily liturgy we remember those whose birthdays are in that month. The back wall of the sanctuary is decorated with seasonal motifs bearing the birthday people's names; those who come are given a corsage and after Mass in the hall we have a birthday cake and coffee.

❑ Children's Liturgy of the Word. Like some other parishes, twice a month at the major Masses we invite the children to the hall for the liturgy of the word and homily. They return to the main church after the homily. It's been helpful and successful.

❑ Sex Education. The cliché is true: the media is the most pervasive sex educator and the most irresponsible one at that. *Newsweek* reports at the end of 1988 that there has been a steady increase in sexual explicitness on television over the years, and that 94 percent of "love in the afternoon" (the soaps) is between partners who are not married, or at least not to each other. As a result, one survey shows that adults, by a two-to-one margin, say that children and teens do not get a realistic understanding of the role of sex in life from watching TV. The Federal Center for Disease Control reports data showing the high promiscuity of young American men; as many as 700,000 of them last year had at least ten sexual partners. The center is alarmed because of the risk of AIDS.

The average public school "health" clinics are Planned Parenthood oriented, if not run, and handing out contraceptives (and often abortion referrals) is the usual procedure for helping the "sexually active." The parochial schols or the parish must step in to assist parents whose values are different from those of the public media and philosophy. Parent support and learning groups are especially valuable, particularly for aiding adolescents. This is the time when this group most needs information but also the time, parents believe, when they are least receptive to getting information from their parents. But psychotherapists who work with teenagers and their families say that those children are listening more closely than they let on. You should know this: in the United States, the average age of first intercourse is 15.7 years for boys and 16.2 for girls, with many instances of the age dropping as low as 12.5 for both sexes. And with such young ages go the devastating traumas of premature pregnancies and the high risk of sexually-transmitted dieases, particularly AIDS. Teens who are at high risk do not realize that they are in special danger because they think of themselves as invincible and because of the long latency period of AIDS, which may not show up for seven to ten years from the time they contract it.

So parents or their trusted surrogates *must* talk with children and teens. For both parents and teens there is that fine videocassette series called "Just Say No" by Josh McDowell: a bit evangelistic, but slick, appealing, and recommended. Parents or the parish might sponsor a speaker like Molly Kast Kelly who talks to kids about chastity and gets standing ovations from them. Share a good textbook series in religious education. Most dioceses and directors of religious education have good resources, and some are listed in this footnote.[3] Remember: significant adults, *especially the parents,* all reports show, still have the major influence on the sexual values and behavior of their children. I can't emphasize this too much. As Dr. Carolyn Maltas, a clinical psychologist at McLean Hospital in Boston, says, "Let your children know what your values are. Adolescents in particular need a set of standards by which they can compare the values they are starting to try on for size. If parents try too hard to accommodate by being 'modern,' it actually makes things more difficult for the adolescent who needs values to grapple with." So parents should get together and search out AIDS programs, and material so they can counteract the public media of exploitation.

❏ Marriage Preparation. We have a seven-step program that has proven helpful. Step 1 is the initial contact with the priest to set time and date and other information. Step 2 is to contact our on-the-premises counselor to begin a long session of testing and preparation. This is the heart of the program. Step 3 assigns the engaged couple a Sponsor Couple, a kind of big brother and sister to meet them, have them over to their house, and just be there for them. Step 4 is a public betrothal ceremony at one of the weekend Masses, for all those intending to be married within the year, so the community may rejoice and pray for them. Step 5 is easy. We have someone mail to each bride and groom little flyers, thought-provokers, fun things that might help them get ready for marriage. Step 6 is the couple's choice of the Pre-Cana Conference or the Engaged Encounter weekend. In step 7, the couple meets with the one who will witness their marriage and coordinate the final details. (They have already been in touch with those in charge of music and flowers.) We also ask them to leave us their new address if they have it so we can contact them in a year or two for a reunion. We have the practical things too: precise written instructions for the photographers and video takers (saves a lot of hassle); bird seed instead of rice (birds sure like it better), words into the mouths of the bride and groom at the beginning of the wedding that they request that, since they have their own photographer, no pictures are to be taken during the ceremony (saves our nerves from the nervy; anyway, we'll be more than happy to re-pose afterwards).

❏ We always have the bride and groom, best man and maid or matron of honor face the congregation during the entire ceremony. The ushers come down the aisle and go into the right front pew, the bridesmaids into the left front pew. The maid or matron of honor joins with the best man (already up front) and they go to the chairs in the sanctuary and face the people, and the bride and groom do the same on the other side of the altar. After the homily, they come down and stand in front of the altar and the ushers and bridesmaids join them so that you have one big chorus line facing the people. After the vows the ushers and bridesmaids are sent back to their places, but the bride and groom and best man and maid or matron of honor join the celebrant at the altar. They remain there until after Communion. Having the wedding party face the people all the time is impressive and intimate and invites a better sense of community at a joyous occasion.

We have the usual other activities, such as bereavement

groups, which meet monthly on Sundays, our senior citizens group, which we call "The Holy Spirits," a mothers' group called M.O.P.I.T.S. (Mothers of Preschool, Infants, Toddlers and School-age children"). They meet once a week (babysitting supplied) for mutual support and company, adult conversation (Mommy, Daddy, and potty only go so far) and discuss a book, watch a video, or listen to a tape or live speaker. We also have couples retreats, spiritual direction for spouses, learning how to meditate and pray for our CCD children, and a high school youth group.

❑ New Drivers' Blessing. Once a year we send out notices to all new drivers (the young people, of course) and invite them and their parents to a Mass. After the homily, the parents and new drivers are invited to the sanctuary where the parents, in possession of the car keys, stand on one side and the young people on the other:

Celebrant:	My dear friends, today we are blessing new drivers and so we pray: Almighty God, Giver of all good gifts, look upon the joy and expectation of the new drivers who are gathered here today. Give them sharpness of eye, keeness of hearing, alertness of mind. But, above all, give them sense and sensitivity, for in a new way precious human life is being entrusted to their care and responsibility. In their work and play, may their driving be both a source of joy and service to us all. May they continually earn the trust of their parents and this community. We ask this through Christ Our Lord. Amen.

Turning to the new drivers, the Celebrant asks them to repeat after him:

Before my parents and my faith community I pledge:
Never to drink and drive,
Never to let anyone who is drinking to drive

my car.
I pledge I will drive safely,
For I know that driving is both a privilege and
a responsibility.
I intend to remember the first and honor the
second,
For all life is precious.
God keep me and my friends safe. Amen.

Now the parents cross over from their side of the sanctuary
and hand the car keys to the new drivers (and give them a
hug!). The Celebrant sprinkles them all with holy water and di-
rects them to return to their pews. (A reference will be made in
the Prayer of the Faithful.)

❏ Down Memory Lane. We have mentioned a bulletin board
in the back of church on which photographs are changed each
month or so according to the liturgical season. Once a year,
however, (or every two or three years if you wish) we have a
weekend devoted to "Memory Lane." This means that we
gather photos and arrange them all around the church. We put
special rectangular boards around all the walls of the church
and on them we fasten as many photographs of people and
events as we can fit—maybe several hundred. If you've been at
a parish ten or more years and people are always taking pictures
(and they should, or you should), then a picture, say, of a group
of CCD kids who were 8 years old are now 18 years old. Adults,
too, are still there and showing maturity. Some may want to
dip into the family album and contribute. In any case, you give
it big publicity and leave the photos up for one or two weekends for all to look at before and after the Masses and during
the week. It's a lot of fun and contributes to family spirit.

❏ Advent and Lent Meditations. During the weeks of advent and lent we ask various people, from oldsters to youngsters, to write a brief meditation or reflection and then we put
them in as a Sunday bulletin insert. It's a chance to get your
name in print and a chance to share some lovely thoughts from
the pew.

❏ Talent Auction. This can be tied in with any fun event. We do this at our annual picnic. We get various people to offer talents or services and then we auction them off to the highest bidder—the proceeds going to charity. Here's one year's sample:

Father Bausch	Will prepare dinner for four; will babysit 2 children overnight in the Parish House. [This was a great one!]
Sister Joan	Luncheon and time at the beach [where she lived] for a person and 1 or 2 friends.
Geri Braden	An afternoon of dog training. [Geri was our youth minister.]
Ralph Imholte	4 tennis lessons. [Ralph is our deacon.]
Maryanne Barone	1 pie a month for a year.
Lorraine Walsh	4 hours of typing.
Carl Baran	Dixieland Band for any occasion.
Lou Schmidt	Create a personalized fragrance. [Lou's a chemist.]

❏ Family Stations. On the Friday evenings of Lent we have families do the stations. They divide among themselves who's going to read the text (a prepared or made-up one), who's going around with the cross and candles, and who's going to say a few words of reflection.

❏ "My Fair Ladies." These days there are many elderly parents living with their married children. Some have attached apartments, others live right in the main house. In either case, such elderly are often lonely (note that the elderly have the nation's largest suicide rate). To help ease the loneliness we have a very simple arrangement called "My Fair Ladies" (with a men's chapter called, appropriately, "The Henry Higginses"). The arrangement is that a group of four or five of them meet once a week in one of the member's homes or apartments for a brown-bag lunch. The host supplies only coffee or tea and maybe a sweet. Their only requirement is that at some point in their being together they recite the Serenity Prayer: God grant me the patience to accept the things I cannot change, the courage to change th ethings I can, and the wisdom to know the difference. For those who need it, our Samaritan groups supplies transportation. Explanation: The brown bag is realistic because so many of them are on restricted diets that they need to bring their own prepared food. Besides, it's easier on the host, who is on a limited income. Limiting the group to four or five persons is also realistic because some of them wear hearing aids and if too many people are talking it's hard for them to sort out and hear.

❑ Coordinator of Cultural Affairs. This sounds like high society, but all it means is that someone (again, for two years) coordinates the parish social life. This position is something like the social director on a cruise. Someone with the knack keeps an eye out for parish fun things that are easy and financially reasonable. For example, our coordinator of cultural affairs had a successful arts display this past year. There was no intent to sell articles, only the intent to have parish people display their talents in the parish. We had photography, oil and watercolor paintings, ceramics, wood carving, caligraphy, needlepoint, and so on. It was a good and revealing family affair. Likewise, such a coordinator can go through all those advertisements a parish receives and work out trips, excursions, plays, theatre, and whatever. It's a neat voluntary position, ready-made for the personality that can help us all enjoy life a little more.

❑ Let's end with a brief fun one: "Mother's Secret Laughter Day." That's the first day of school when both kids and parents are nervous and mothers especially are weeping as they take their children to school. But inside, ah, inside there is laughter. Yes, they love their kids, but just think, five hours of freedom, of uninterrupted time. So, like Sarah, they laugh secretly and we celebrate that. We invite them all over to the parish—at least those not working outside the home—after they drop the kids off, to talk, have a continental breakfast, and, yes, despite the apprehension, to laugh a little.

CHAPTER 13

Parish Booklet
and Planning

Every year we publish a parish booklet. It's not necessary to do so and some parishes publish a monthly calendar in their Sunday bulletin, which allows for greater flexibility. Besides, a parish booklet can be expensive. So why do we do it? There are several reasons.

1. Meeting the printing deadline forces us to plan ahead. We begin right after Easter. All during the year we have been popping ideas into our idea box in the common office, and now we look at them. We gather an ad hoc committee of random parishioners and put all the ideas from the box, from the staff, from anybody, on newsprint. Then we talk about them, solicit new ideas, pare down the list, and come up with a tentative theme. Then we take this to the parish council for further discussion and approval. But most of all, the very deadline of a parish

booklet (we try to get it to the printers by the first week of July so people can get it in the mail before Labor Day) forces us to plan and to line up speakers and volunteers. This is the time when my famous (infamous) letters go out asking different people if they would chair this or that, help out with this or that, be on this or that committee. (Remember, people are susceptible to saying yes when the event or task is so distant in time.)

❑ Letters From the Pastor. The pastor still has enough mystique that people don't like to refuse him. Furthermore, it's gratifying to get a personal letter from the pastor asking this or that. It certainly suggests that he knows you and thinks you have something to offer. I think of the 50 or 60 letters that go out at this time, with only about two refusals. I try to make refusing easy. Here's a sample letter:

Dear Bill and Winifred:

Each year, as you may know, we have a Lenten Communal Confession. This coming year it will be held on Tuesday evening, April 10.

I'm writing to ask if you two would host this particular event. Actually, it's not difficult. It just means setting up the church by putting some chairs in the sanctuary, and providing a little coffee and cookies afterwards when it's over. It begins at eight o'clock and is over by nine.

The people who ran it last year will be glad to assist you, and if you accept I'll have them contact you.

It's not difficult, but it is a beautiful and moving ceremony and we just need someone in charge. I realize that you may not be able to help out this time and I surely understand that, but if you could, I and the parish community would be most grateful. So let me know if you're able to do this and thanks for being members of our parish.

Sincerely yours,

The parish booklet committee also calls all the organizations and gets an update on membership and leaders for inclusion in the booklet. All this is genuinely hard and intensive work, but it's all worth it. It's nice, by the middle of summer, to know that next year is all planned: calendar, speakers, events, activities, and, most of all, volunteers. They're all signed up already! Sure, there'll be changes and adjustments, but at least we have something to adjust *from*.

2. The specter of a parish booklet deadline forces the organizations and ministries to do their planning. I send all the leaders a letter announcing that next year's calendar from September to June is now (in April or May) posted on the walls of the parish hall. Do your planning and get your dates and events marked in. First come, first choice. This posted calendar has a great negative value. It helps to iron out conflicts then and there. If one organization is planning a dance and sees one already marked in nearby or on the same day, that organization can adjust. Actually, there will be standard calendar events: Christmas and Easter, for example; plus our annual activities such as an Advent and Lenten communal confession, first communion, senior citizens' days of recollection, the annual picnic, CCD classes, pre-cana and so on. We then add the variables, such as courses, lectures, plays, meeting nights, days and evenings of recollection, socials, and all the rest.

3. Mailing a parish booklet gives the parishioners a chance to look things over and save time for the events they want to attend. They can sense a certain rhythm and flow to the year. Fourth, as I hinted before, the booklet, with its theme and dedication, gives a certain amount of identity and cohesion to the parish and a sense that we have a purpose and know where we're going (even when that's not quite true).

The parish booklet is divided into seven sections that reflect the fullness of our life together. It seems to me that these seven sections might also offer the elements of a successful parish.

Section 1 is "Learning." Before we can love God we must know God. So this section deals with our full adult education offerings—everything from courses and lectures to bible study groups and midlife workshops. Included as well are the children's programs, from religious education to Vacation Bible school.

❏ A.M. Table Talks. This is a 10:00 A.M. gathering (hence it leaves out those working outside the home, but we tried a P.M. Table Talk and it didn't work; this one has.) We sell tickets for $3.00 and this entitles one to a continental breakfast (at round tables attractively prepared) and a fine speaker on a topic that is near to the hearts of people: relationship topics, children, spouses, friendship, and personal growth. We have these Table Talks every other month and they have gone over very well.

Section 2 is "Worshiping," loving the God we know. This section includes our parish Mass schedule (with its variety of High Mass, Folk Mass, Mass with Children, etc.) plus the Mass schedules of all of the surrounding parishes. It also includes other liturgical and spiritual activities such as May crowning, stations of the cross, prayer groups, spiritual direction, retreats, recollections, holy hours, spiritual reading, and Anointing Mass. This section also includes the names, addresses, and phone numbers of nearby retreat houses and houses of prayer.

❏ Included here is also a valuable subsection: our sacramental policies, all spelled out. It's so much better to have the parish's policies on marriage, funeral, baptism, and the like all down in black and white so there's neither surprise on the people's part (for example, that couples have to give at least 8 months notice for a wedding or have to attend prebaptismal classes) nor angst on our part in having to play each and every situation by ear (for example, do we bury suicides?).

Section 3 is entitled "Helping." It lists all the helps that the parish community offers from AIDS hotline, Gamblers' Anonymous, Frozen meals, Lazarus, nullities, etc. to the helps that the larger communities offer Marriage Encounter, Pentecostal or charismatic groups, drug problems, divorced and separated, pregnancy counseling, etc.

Section 4 is called "Playing" and lists our parish social life: events, date, place (concerts, picnic, bowling, dances, bridge, trips, plays, etc.).

Section 5 is "Organizing," and it lists all of the parish organizations and ministries, members and volunteers (loads of them), with the phone numbers of the leaders. It mentions everyone who is doing something, from this year's neighborhood Christmas decorating group, to the keeper of the Guest book, to the flower arrangers to the altar bread bakers.

Section 6 is called "Exploring" because in this section we list all the new things we're going to try this year. Some are successful and so become part of our normal pattern; others are a disaster and we let them die a natural death. Many of the permanent ideas in this book started out in this section.

Finally, our last section, Section 7, is called "Unfolding" and is our parish calendar, about 15 pages listing everything that's happening on a particular day. The parish booklet closes with an index. Its opening pages give a list of vital information at a glance plus an introduction to the staff and the theme and dedication.

The booklet is attractive with nice clip-art visuals. Some may find the whole concept too rigid or regimented, but we are flexible and are ready to make adjustments where needed and when required. I still think it's better to know now when next year's Advent communal confession is and who's in charge than to run around a month before asking about it; better to have an overall picture than to fly by the seat of your pants.

❑ Adjunct Members. Every organization has its standard members and it tends to use these members exclusively. And then they wonder why they can't get others involved. Those "others" get the impression that everything's taken care of or that some people don't want to let go. So I give all the organizations a list of new and usual people and urge them that, for every five to ten usual members on some activity, they should solicit one different person from the list to help out. They must be very careful not to try to recruit. They're just asking for help on this one project. They have to gamble whether or not the adjunct person will want to become more interested. This play has the advantage of pulling in new people on what amounts to a trial basis and breaking (somewhat) the hold the usual people have—those who complain that there's no one to do anything anymore but who unconsciously set the barriers against help.

❑ "Happy Endings." One of the minor problems of every parish is precisely those wonderful and competent people who have both the time and the talent to do so many things. And the parish would be lost without them. Still, the parish is larger than this group and something must be done to get others involved. Our policy of "happy endings" means that no one may hold an office for more than two years (with obvious specialist exceptions such as organists, religious education teachers, etc.), but must step down into the ranks or move into some other ministry. In fact, the leader must prepare his or her replacement. This policy keeps cliques from hardening and widens the involvement. And, of course, it *is* easier to get volunteers if they know that they will not be stuck in the job for the next century, have to sell their house, and never see their grandchildren.

CHAPTER 14

A Vestibule
Full of Ideas

Here, pulled together, are additional ideas—about 20 of them—that help create parish spirit. I have three concerns about these ideas and the others scattered throughout the previous chapters.

1. Some people might think them merely clever. I think we have a minor horror of doing things out of mere cleverness (remember, our parish council keeps us honest), the horror that form might overshadow substance, and cuteness might substitute for the gospel. We don't want to get caught in the "aren't-we-a-wonderful-parish" posture while the greater issues of justice and mercy go begging. God deliver us from that.

2. I don't want people to think that any of the ideas expressed in this book are merely duplicable. Some are, some

aren't. Some will soar, others will sink. As the *Music Man* singers put it, "You gotta know the territory." Still, these ideas, kept within context, are truly helpful and even the frivolous ones can add a bit of pizazz to parish life.

3. Some parishes don't know when to put things away. Ideas and programs, marvelous at one time, tend to run a natural course and often grow wearisome or, at times, counterproductive. Yet, because "we've always done it this way," they linger on eventually to burden rather than enhance the parish. And, let's also face it, ideas and programs, marvelous at one time, can tumble into ignominious failure at another. But I've found that Americans in general, and Catholics in particular, have a fear of failure. This or that idea or organization is dead and nobody will bury it—expecially if it's the pastor's or "significant other's" idea or program. We find it hard to say, "This idea or organization or society did a great service. We are what we are because of it. It has helped us to grow and so now we're ready to move on, to go in new directions. How grateful we are for their groundwork." For some strange reason that escapes me, a society that has done fifty years of great service but no longer functions is called a "failure." I am always amazed when people declare the dinosaurs a "failure," disappearing as they did after some few million years. We should all be such "failures"! No, such societies or organizations are grand successes, a link in our growth—a growth beyond what they seeded. Perhaps every five years a parish ought to bring in a few outside consultants to take a neutral look and help in the pruning process, pruning dead programs that are draining the energy that should go in new directions.

Anyway, with this preamble in mind, here's a pocketful of ideas.

❑ Telecare. This is good to do every four or five years. We split up the parish list and ask each participant to call every parishioner twice during the year. There are no strings attached. This is just a way to get to everyone, especially those who usually fall between the cracks. The callers are trained to say that they're calling on behalf of the parish just to let the persons know we're thinking of them. If any serious responses start to come, the callers are not to handle them. Instead, they pleasantly make a referral to the proper person. For example, if someone on the other end of the line starts to talk about his or her second marriage, the caller refers that person to the one in charge of nullities or our marriage counselor. This is a wonderful project for the elderly and the shut-ins who need to feel needed. It has worked for us, a minor but well received outreach, a pleasant "How are you?" from the parish. Naturally, in this, as in all else, we give sufficient advertising of what we're doing.

❏ Raffle of Pastor, Associate. We have a raffle with the religious education kids (or school kids). Their names are placed in a raffle cage and whosever name is picket out wins the pastor. The student takes home a form letter (with a penciled in date and time) telling the parents of the "prize." The letter is quite diplomatic and leaves plenty of room for the parents to beg off. The proposed meeting is usually an early evening, cup-of-coffee visit. It is short a and neat way to get to know the people. Here's the letter:

Dear Parents,

Your child won (or lost, depending on how you look at it) a Nice Prize and a Strange Prize in my class raffle.

The Nice Prize is a nice gift which I hope your child has shown you. The Strange Prize is—me! Yes, we had a drawing at the class I had with the children and the name drawn (your child's, as it happens) got the gift and me along with it.

That is to say, as your child hands you this, I will come and visit your home on the date and time written below.

I usually will come early and stay only about 10 or 15 minutes because I have evening appointments and you have other things to do. But the point is that I just wanted to drop by, see where you live, meet the family and have a cup of coffee. That's all. Please don't clean or fuss (bachelors like me don't notice things).

I fully realize that the time and date I've listed below may be inconvenient, so please don't hesitate to postpone or cancel altogether. I surely will understand. I just wanted this to be a gesture to you and you child, to show interest and care, and mostly I want to know your child by name and face and to be his or her friend.

Thanks for reading this. Much peace and prayer.

Sincerely yours,
Father Bausch

I will come and visit your house on _____, at _____ P.M. If this is not convenient, call me at 780-2666 and leave word.

❑ Epiphany Kings. On Epiphany Sunday we have adults lurking at the church vestibule with fabulous gowns and headpieces (left over from the children's Christmas Mass) waiting to invite the children as they come in to be kings at that liturgy. They are dressed, process in with the presider and ministers, stay up in the sanctuary, and act as offertory gift-bearers. It is a small gesture, but a pleasant surprise for the children and their families, and it gives local color for a colorful feast.

❑ Epiphany Map. This has more to do with the homilists, but it's a good (on occasion) object lesson. I place a large world map on an easel. After an introduction about the meaning of Epiphany and that we're here in this country because that initial Lukan theme of universal salvation personified by the Gentile Magi is realized in our ancestors who came to this land, I asked around the congregation, who has roots in: Poland, Germany, Japan, Italy, etc. As each one stands up or responds to the country of origin I name, I put a map pin into that country. Before long, of course, you have many pins, many countries, and so you draw the object of how far that Epiphany message has spread even to right here and now in this time and place and parish. I remember one year, after I called out all the countries and got all the responses, that I said, "Well, that's it." That's when one lady raised her hand and said I forgot one country. What was that? Where was her ancestry from? She called out simply, "American Indian." I rejoined, "Foreigner!"

❑ Priests' Monthly Schedule. Because I'm the only resident priest in the parish (we have a priest come in for weekend help), I work on the principle that both the clergy and the people should have a sense of schedule. I don't believe that the pastor should always have the same Mass *per omnia saecula saeculorum. Amen.* The people deserve better than that. For years I myself had enough of not knowing what Mass I had until near midnight Saturday. So we rotate on a monthly basis. One priest has the same Masses for one month and we switch the next month. This gives the clergy a chance to savor all the Masses (and each has its distinct personality) and vice versa. It also gives a nice chance to develop a theme for four or five weekends, and it gives the priest a perfect projection for the future. He'll always know which Mass he has.

❑ Crosses at Passiontide. We had fifteen families make man-size crosses (following a pattern made for us by a carpenter) and during passiontide we erect them strung out on our twenty-five acres. They make a powerful silhouette from the nearby highway that's in front of our property. We have Stations of the Cross at 3:00 P.M. on Good Friday and, even in bad weather, we usually draw from 1100 to 1300 people. We have a strong set of participation prayers and a choir that follows a car-drawn PA system. During the Stations acolytes go around and give each person a small wooden cross with a purple string. (We get them from a Newman Club from a midwest college that makes these crosses as a money-raising project). It's wonderful witness to those driving by to see that mob there (again the power of "cult). Having twenty-five acres helps, but even in an inner city, those stations could be placed or painted on the alleys and byways and made to identify even more with the "cry of the poor."

❑ Telephone Sticker. Speaking of money raisers, an easy one is to have a small sticker made with emergency telephone numbers on it that can be placed on a telephone. These stickers can be sold or given to all, and are very handy.

❑ Decorate Father's Tree. Like everyone else, I enjoy Christmas and put up a Christmas tree—an old six-foot failing artificial one. But why do it alone? So we have a raffle for the fifth and sixth graders. They can buy a chance for five cents—the proceeds go to charity—a chance for the privilege of decorating Father's tree. (Get a whiff of Tom Sawyer here?) We have a drawing and the winners are the first five names drawn from the fifth grade and five names from the sixth. At a predetermined time they come to the parish house. We have a great time putting up the tree and that's followed by games and refreshments (and my straightening it out when they leave).

❑ Poinsettias for Christmas. During the Christmas season we go around and give a poinsettia to every family who has lost someone in death during this year. We also give a short letter with it:

Dear Friend,

We know that during this past year you have lost a family member and that therefore this Christmas will be a little less joyous. The season will sharpen the memories.

Still, we wanted you to know that you are not alone, that we your parish family remember you in a special way at this time.

So please accept this poinsettia as a token of our concern and a gesture of our sympathy and love.

Sincerely yours,
The People at St. Mary's

❑ Spaghetti Video. This might have less power now that everybody has a VCR. But we offer a grand combination for $6.00 for adults and $3.00 for kids: a full spaghetti dinner with all the trimmings followed by a family (VCR) movie in our theatre. It's a nice treat.

❑ Cracker Barrel. This reflects the old New England town meeting. Once a year we invite anyone to come to our parish hall, which is strewn with hay and peanut shells. We offer refreshments, and give people an opportunity just to talk with the pastor and anyone on the staff about anything whatsoever, from the serious to the silly, from compliment to complaint. It's a kind of "20/20" Barbara Walters special. The last Cracker Barrel meeting we had was entitled, "Why I Am Not a Monsignor" and drew a good crowd who wanted a first-hand report of my bumpy career of tilting with the powers that be.

❑ Suggestion Box. We have a suggestion box in the foyer of the church. It gives people, native or visitors, a chance to pop an idea into our heads. Last week we found a suggestion from a visitor: Why don't you leave extra Sunday bulletins around for visitors? Why not? So now we do. The suggestion box is not over-used, but its presence, its symbol, is important.

❑ Public Bulletin Board. We have a large cork board in our foyer onto which any reasonable notice may be hung. It's a public service and indicates that we, too, are a part of the community.

❑ Name Tags. One year we made a big to-do about getting to know each other. So we mailed every family a couple of name tags and had the ushers with extra ones at the church door. We asked the people to wear them from September to November and to look boldly at each other's names ("The face I know, but can't put a name on it."). We had fun with this, and it really did help.

❑ Vacation Map. Before the summer began we asked people to mail a card (with greetings and name) to the parish from their vacation destination. Then we put a large world map on the bulletin board in the back of the church. As we received the cards, we stapled them around the map like a large border and then ran a wool thread from the card and pinned the other end to the place they visited. It was great fun seeing the map fill up and families find out where each other had gone, and hearing them squeal with delight if they visited the same place.

❑ Overnight Kids' Retreat. We have the fifth-grade boys and girls take turns at an overnight retreat at the parish house.

We limit it to 15. The kids bring their sleeping bags and arrive around 7:00 P.M. We have a program of films, discussion, prayer, and play and then they bed down in the parish house basement (which is finished off) in one large room. After the pillow fights, they eventually get to sleep. The next day we have a prayer ceremony and breakfast at McDonalds. Then, around 10:00 A.M. they're picked up by the parents. We try to get popular people to give the retreats. We have no illusions whatsoever that the kids are there for religion. They're there to kill each other with pillows. That's O.K. What we're after is the association, the memory. Did you ever spend an overnight at the rectory or convent? These days, especially when both tend to be quite empty, this venture might be a way to get to know the kids and a way to build some closeness.

❏ Agape. On the last Sunday of every month after the main Mass we have our agape: free coffee, cider and donuts for everyone. The various organizations are lined up to host them.

❏ Welcome Wagon. Our township sends us a list of all new residents. They are then visited by our Welcome Wagon crew who give them a packet containing our parish booklet and the Covenant plus other civic and church information.

❏ Soup 'n Song. As a parish we make the Tuesdays of Lent our special day of emphasis. We start the day with the 6:30 A.M. men's Divine Office, have Mass at 9:00 and Soup 'n Song at noon. This event is for the working folk. They come to church for a brief service: opening hymn and prayer, Scripture and reflection followed by Benediction. Then off to the parish hall. Three different neighborhoods have made homemade soup and bread. We get the high school kids released from the local Catholic high schools to serve the meal as part of their lenten service. Then, whatever money the people might have paid for a regular lunch is put into a box for the unemployed. Finally, in the evening there is a Holy Hour from 8:00 to 9:00.

❏ Mail Slot. In our church vestibule (which is not that large) we have a side door that leads from the sacristy. We presume this door was put there as an escape route for the priest: out the side door to the outside door to safety! We have a main sacristy door that exits right into church, so we don't use that side, "into-the-vestibule" door. We keep it locked and have put a mail slot in it over which is the sign: "Please drop here all book rack money, returns, replies, responses, etc." We're always having something that needs a reply and on the weekends when most people come to church it's handy to have a mail slot right in the vestibule for them.

❏ Saturday Night Dinners. Since I don't have a housekeeper and do all my own cooking, every Saturday night (except in the summer) I have two couples in for dinner (couples being married, widows, singles, etc.). It's been a most satisfying way to meet people and a real "breaking of bread" that builds community.

❏ Teaching Mass. Every year or two, there ought to be a teaching Mass, one that is explained in "slow motion." In an ecumenical spirit you might, as we did, invite our separated brethren. But even Catholics have been most enthusiastic in getting a good review of what their central act of worship is all about. (Good background: *This Is Our Mass* by Tom Coyle, Twenty-Third Publications).

❏ Anointing at Mass. In keeping with our policy of celebrating all of the sacraments with and by the community, we have the celebration of the sacrament of the sick during the community Mass. An added touch is that we invite the caregiving community to participate: doctors, nurses, aids, and the local first aid squad. Their presence and an acknowledgment of their great usefulness and service is a must.

❏ Blessing of the Pets. Like many other places, we bless people's pets on or near the feast of St. Francis. We hold it outdoors at our St. Francis meditation garden since we have horses come, but it could be done indoors for the smaller pets. The celebrant dresses up like St. Francis with sandals and beard (grown or pasted on for the occasion) and an artificial bird sewn on top of the shoulder helps. We also bless bicycles on this occasion.

❏ Storytelling for "Widowed" Times. By this I mean that when all or most of males have slipped off the planet to watch non-stop Superbowl, the parish holds a storytelling festival at the parish for the survivors—mostly the wives and children. They love it and it is well attended. About two hours (with breaks) will do. If none of the staff is comfortable with this, have someone from the local library tell or read some terrific stories (or at least give you sources. Your DRE will be helpful here.).

❑ The Affirmation Affair. This we borrowed and modified from another parish. That parish has a parochial grammar school and the religious director there had the students write letters to all of the priests of the diocese, letters designed to reach them before Holy Thursday, congratulating them and thanking them for dedicating their lives to the service of God and his people. Many of the priests thrilled the youngsters by responding. Since we don't have a school, we have adapted as follows: we have our Polaris group (young adults from 18 to 35) write similar letters to all of our religious education teachers, coordinators, and directors, likewise thanking them for their dedication. Another variation is that we have the children in CCD write to all of the teachers in the local parochial and public schools along the same lines. Obviously, the list is nigh endless.

Every parish has its way of making things human and these are some of ours. Not all are necessarily the best, and individually one or other may be quite tepid. I think, however, that we must look at the cumulative effect, so that a person even dropping into an empty church on a visit receives a mighty message and notices lots of little in-place things that say, Welcome, people live and worship here, that, as the saying on our colored balloons has it, "The Spirit Is Alive at St. Mary's."

CHAPTER 15

How Do You Do It, Pay for It?

You might suspect that this is easier to ask than to answer. It's like trying to define love: you can't do it justice. Something gets lost in the dissecting. So when people ask how do you do it, I'm not sure of my answer, since "doing it" has such a history of struggle and uncertainty. Besides, as I indicated in the preface, I'm deeply conscious that I'm speaking from a limited experience, reflecting a middle to upper white middle-class suburban church with certain givens, for example, a certain level of education. I don't know what I would do with the parish that has decayed, whose aging building is nearly empty on the weekends, whose original clientele has long ago given way to various ethnic groups, many of whom do not speak English, where unemployment is rampant and crack is sold in the streets. Yes, some would find a way to gather a faith community and many have, but that is their genius, not mine. I can only stand back in awe and admiration, and make room for them and learn from them.

On the other hand, mine is typical of many other parishes, and to them I can speak. To the question of how you do it (go about building community, get people involved), I can respond with four categories. First and foremost (for me) has been education. I don't mean that you want to form a university of theological elites, but you should want a parish that understands itself and who and what it is. Some will relish such education and become more sophisticated, others will care less, but all will benefit in some broad way from being educated as to who they are as Christians. The reason for placing such a high priority on education is that people really don't understand the changes made by Vatican II. No one has told them why and wherefore or given them the broader view. People still equate Catholicism with their very limited experience of it (and identify with the institutional side, not the lived side). They are ignorant of the vast riches and variety of the Catholic tradition. They can't even criticize the changes (some of which surely deserve criticism) because they haven't the background. They just know something's wrong and the drastic drop in Sunday Mass attendance is its own commentary. As one English mother has written:

> We are a family of eight, now reduced to three church-goers.... What happened? Some vignettes.
> Eldest son—who since his first communion has gone every month, without prompting, to confession—sitting with his friend at the feet of the Jesuit successor to our old parish priest, both boys looking up to him with hero worship. Our future priests? I remember wondering. The Jesuit was taken away after one year, his successor after another. The boys do not go to church anymore. "Too many changes" my son said. "You get put off somehow."
> Eldest daughter on hearing that our team ministry was to

modernize the church that she had attended: "Oh no. They'll spoil it. They'll take away the pews as they've done in the other." They did...

Second son. "You do realize, Mum, that I'm the only squaddie in Catterick who goes to Mass on a Sunday?" I think perhaps he goes still, but when he comes home now, the liturgy and the places of his Catholic youth have no reassuring familiarity.

My oldest daughter has just been confirmed. Part of her preparation required her to deliver parish envelopes over quite a large area....

My husband, well, it was not very nice of him to shout at the elderly nun about her taste in hymns—the words, if I remember correctly, had to do with being a fuzzy bear and praising the Lord....

Myself? I have wept: when I have seen a gaping hole in the brickwork where the great stone altar stood; when instead of silence at the heart of the Mass it became all chant and response, and even straight after communion the human voice broke briskly in....I only occasionally protest at the English: "Greetings, Mary—you are pregnant."[1]

Whether or not we agree with this mother, we can still sense that she's on to something. Something is missing. A whole culture that she knew was reduced to and translated into English—a banal English at that—and it shouldn't be done. She or her husband or children do not understand why they do not see the gain or feel the old impulse anymore.

We must patiently teach so that we can all validate together what has truly been movement, expansion, and progress and change together what has been wrong-headed or simply not workable. In the practical realm that means that when I first came to the parish I gave a lot of explanation to the largest single audience I could find: the Sunday congregation. I know the purists say you must always preach a homily on the Scripture and I concur. It's just that, as St. Paul would say, how can people know God's word unless they are preached to? How can they be preached to unless they are first prepared (evangelized)? So I took time systematically to explain the history, the origins, the development of the spirit and proposals of Vatican II and help the people see themselves as church. (The first chapters of this book have been broken down and given from the pulpit.) I tried to do this gently so that those who disagreed would not feel left out or less Catholic. I refused to make anything either-or: either you have communal confession or you have the green scapular. It's a large church and should be big enough to contain both.

Simultaneously, I used bulletin inserts that dovetailed with my explanations. Some I did myself; others were excellent, prepackaged, one- or two-page flyers, such as the *St. Anthony Messenger* "Updates." We find that such inserts get read. Then I gave formal courses in the evenings for those who wished to come.

In addition to these "head" items, we practiced a "hands-on" approach. People got involved and had to know what they were doing and the theology behind, say, a communal confession or a prebaptism class. As I mentioned before, we sent people away to workshops and seminars and to other parishes that were doing things well. I also found training booklets a great help. We used to mimeograph (before computers and printouts) tons of stuff and paste in pictures, run them off and them staple them into attractive and useful booklets for anything from the blessing of ashes and pets to paraliturgical celebrations of Advent or Christmas. The idea was to give a complete booklet with an explanatory introduction, music (got permission), scripture, text, and directions all built right from beginning to end so that people could follow along in one single motion. Thus, the booklet itself became a great teaching tool, a model of how it's done. We did lots and lots of these booklets in the early years and it took a lot of work, but gradually we were able to realize our goal. People learned and eventually got rid of the booklets. Our policy of the "Glenmary dance" and leadership turnover ("Happy Endings") every two years has helped democratize the learning. It took about six to seven years of such education to get a solid base.

❏ With the ease of a personal computer and printer you can rather cheaply produce attractive booklets and either put them together yourself or give the local printer the finished product to print and bind. We have small booklets for: Stations of the Cross (for the more than 1000 persons who participate), the Lazarus committee (such booklets have readings, music, prayers, and serve as a common Mass text as well as a memento for the family), Passion Sunday (has the script for mutual reading of the Passion), Grotto Devotions, eucharistic ministers' booklet, and even a "Now and Then" booklet, which pulls together odds and ends that we need at different times. The value of these booklets (again nicely done with clip art), is that they have what you need under one cover, and there's no reason to juggle all kinds of missalettes and texts and song books. They're handy, disposable, and easily stored until you need them.

❏ The second category of "how-to-do-it" is involvement. And to this end I seldom ask for volunteers (called my "RSVP principle"). Right now, if you advertise in your Sunday bulletin for volunteers, you could write the names of 80 percent of those who come forward on a piece of paper beforehand. As I mentioned in an earlier chapter, I invite. Inviting gives me a chance to mix people who don't know one another and coax out those who would never volunteer. It gives me a chance to broaden the hands-on experience. The pastor still has enough mystique that people don't like to refuse him. And note that in the process the invitees are taught and trained by last year's volunteers, thus exhibiting our "piggy-back" principle. That principle is the second half of our fuller "one-shot, piggy-back" principle. That means that we ask someone to do something "just one time, just one event, for example, the Advent Communal Confession. When it's all over, that person can recede into the faceless crowd. (Often, however, they're "caught.") The one-time task is attractive in getting people to do things, as is the "piggy-back" which means that last year's people will walk with and assist this year's people and this year's people have the obligation to work with and assist next year's people. Sooner or later, you get a cache of trainers in the parish.

The third category is language. We've all become sensitized to inclusive language. Likewise, we should become sensitized to language's power to narrow or widen the content of community and ministry and "ownership." For instance, whenever visitors look around our worship space and exclaim, "Oh, what a beautiful church!" my stock reply is, "Yes, and the building is nice too." (Are the people the church or not? We, of course, continue to use the word church in its usual popular context—we're not that esoteric—but we prefer to use it in reference to people.) If you meet one of our parishioners and exclaim, "Oh, you belong to Father Bausch's parish," you're just as likely to get the retort, "No, he belongs to my parish." I don't even like using the phrase "going to church." It sounds too much like going to a club. Rather, the church gathers, or, we're gathering for worship. We don't use terms such as rectory, but we have a parish church, a parish hall, a parish spiritual center, a parish house. In the same way, instead of "Rosary Altar Guild" we have a "Martha/Mary Guild" (action-contemplation); instead of a "social justice committee" we have an "Assisi Group" (How can you get mad at Francis?). We don't have "senior citizens" but the "Holy Spirits." The visuals are pronounced: large bread used at the eucharist, strong cruets for the wine and water, the Bible enthroned as you enter the church, the font in a prominent place, striking banners. So the language we use is itself educational.

The final category is, as we indicated previously, lowering the barriers: keys, locks, doors, materials, etc. are all accessible. This invites a hands-on participation, a learning experience as a "being" experience. So does our one-shot, piggy-back approach—personally inviting people rather than seeking volunteers, giving people a gracious way to say no or to leave after a certain amount of time, and using language that expresses our vision of parish. Most of all, to me, teaching is important as a means of building community, teaching combined with doing. This is a hands-on parish.

How about one of those intriguing statistical tidbits right here just to break things up? This is from the Notre Dame Study of Catholic Parish Life, which showed that almost 65 percent of parishioners are involved in either their parish or community, and that the one fact most closely associated with parish involvement is Bible reading! That surprised me, but I pass it on for what it's worth. As the researchers said:

> We have much data on Catholic devotional practices. The fascinating conclusion is that no other private or public devotional practice does a better job of predicting parish involvement that does the frequency of Bible reading.... We cannot say that Bible reading causes involvement; perhaps involvement causes Bible reading. What we can say is that the two are part of the same complex and that they have positive effects on each other.

So Bible study groups may do more good than you think.

So, now the big one: How do you pay for all this? Do you have a budget? Who keeps the books? First of all, we have no school so any monies can go into total parish programming. That's a critical statement, as most pastors know, and I want to explore it, for it symbolizes a deeper concern. For more than a quarter of a century I have been arguing that no parish should have a parochial school—nor a hospital for that matter. Before you react, let me say that I am very much in favor of parochial schools and I am distressed that the bishops have lost their collective nerve about them. The schools have proven to be most effective in creating positive attitudes, less prejudice, more respect and for the most part an excellent education. However, my contention has been and is that the school should be centralized on the public school model. It should be run from a central office which can regulate schedules, benefits, hiring and firing, union challenges, etc. in a professional, consistent way. Most of all, a centralized diocesan system frees the parish of the problems of divisiveness. Any parish school automatically creates an us-them mentality. It can't be helped. It polarizes the "Catholic school" kids and the CCD kids and their parents. Often the school becomes the focal point of parish life, the money-maker, the social center. It takes up to 60-70 percent of the parish budget. And, more ominously, it takes a great deal of time and energy of the pastor or pastoral assistant who, in fact, may or may not be an educator.

When I see parishes running four to six bingos a week to keep the school afloat, my first reaction is one of sympathy, for I know they need the money. But my other reaction is one of distress because no one is stepping back and asking, What are we doing? What is a parish for? Have we become a "plant" so devoted to maintaining the institution that we have no time for growth? Surely we have here the financial tail wagging the community dog. All that energy to raise school money! What about the rest of the parish, other segments, the youth, family life, *adult* education, and so on? What about those rooms used for bingo that therefore are not, cannot be, used for other community, spiritual-building events? If things are that desperate for the school, might we not have to rethink our priorities or perhaps close the whole complex down and figure out what we're about, what gospel message we're giving, or failing to give? The school is really too much, too divisive, too unbalancing for the average parish to handle. We need a better school (and hospital) policy that respects not only the financial realities but, more importantly, the faith community realities. We need a more prophetic stance that challenges our devotion to one institution at the expense of the whole people of God.

Someone recently told me a story after my own heart. A priest in New Guinea was twice elected bishop and twice refused, until Rome stepped in and ordered him to take the job. He assented under the condition—which was granted—that he could do it his way. So he called for a three-year moratorium for his diocese! That is, he shut everything down and told the people to take three years to discover what kind of church they wanted to be. Ultimately their answer was to restructure along gospel lines and come up with three hundred base communities. At the first convocation the delegates of these three hundred base communities gathered and they asked the bishop for the meeting's agenda. He replied by opening up the Bible to "The Acts of the Apostles" and said, "Here's our agenda, here's where we begin."

For me it's a thrilling story of a prophet trying to come to terms with gospel priorities, brushing the buildings aside to get at the heart of the matter. I always have this fantasy that someday some newly made bishop in the United States would do that: shut down the entire diocese for a period while we all go and pray and study the gospels and rediscover who we are. Anyway, I put the New Guinea story in the same category as recent policy of Bishops Hunthausen and Murphy from Seattle. They had the boldness and honesty to make it a public policy that when a parish is open they will put in the most competent person as pastor—whether layman or cleric for, as they expressed it, they "no longer wish to reward incompetency." So, when you ask about money and my first long homily is that I don't have a school, what I'm really trying to tell you is that, while I'm greatly in favor of the Catholic school, not having one enables me to put an overall thrust to the entire parish family; that my energies are not divided and money is not divided, but that we can meet composite, total needs of all the people without compromise or prejudice.

So, to continue. For one thing, many of the things we do, many of the ideas you're read so far, in fact need little money and so there's no financial problem in taking care of them. Moreover, I said that we were in the middle to upper middle-income area. That does help—certainly it must be difficult for many inner-city parishes—but even so, that's absolutely no guarantee of an adequate collection. Other factors are far more critical. As Andrew Greeley points out, American Catholics are the wealthiest in the world, but in spite of that their giving is down. In 1960, Catholics and Protestants both gave 2.2 percent. By 1985, Protestants were still giving 2.2 percent, but Catholics had declined to 1.1 percent, which in practical terms is equivalent to a $6 billion loss a year. So the question is, if Catholics have more money than ever, why do they give less than ever? Greeley's data (and I agree with his analysis of it) shows that the decline is due to voting with the purse strings; that is, people don't like a lot of things that are happening in the church and are simply protesting the only way they know how—or are allowed to—by holding back their money. That's the bottom line: people are angry and are showing it.[2] Is there an answer to this? Yes, according to Greeley: the solution is sharing with the people the decision about how money is raised and how it is spent. In short, share fiscal power. It's as simple as that.

There's good sense to this. People are sharp and they want a say in serious matters. Having a shared and collaborative ministry, a sense of co-responsibility, of ownership, and lots of say in the parish gives people a vested interest in it—and an "investing" interest. I think that's why they give and why we can operate in the black. And that's also why we never talk money here, take no stipends (except for Masses), and have one and only one collection at each Sunday Mass, no matter what, and none on holy days. Nor do we ever allow the buying and selling of chances or tickets, etc. before or after Mass. As I wrote in *The Christian Parish*:

>...unfitting distractions should not overlay the main purpose of what the parish is about when it meets to pray publicly...People should not always be meeting benign vendors on their way in or out waving chances in their faces for the latest color TV or car—especially if the Scripture readings for that particular weekend have been prophetically disturbing about our many commercial idols, or the anawim of the Old Testament who are the Boat People of today.

There's something about a gorgeous Lincoln Continental gloriously displayed in front of the church to elicit oohs and aahs that says, No matter what goes on inside about God,

Mammon rules the outside. It's a competing icon.

People can look at the books any time. A financial committee takes care of them and I have nothing to do with the money—I neither count it nor bank it. As a legal administrator, I sign the checks that are put before me, but that is all. The people get a financial report. There are no money secrets here. As a baptized parishioner, by the way, I also receive envelopes and I am the first one the usher comes to with the basket at collection time. Anyway, if people know you're working for them and see that the money is going somewhere and is not being buried or siphoned off on frivolous things, they will respond.

There's another source of money that might not be too impressive until you think about it. It's the negative source: that is, the money we *don't* spend because of volunteerism. We'll ask individuals to use their talents or resources to do or fix things. When it snows the farmer comes over with a front end loader and cleans off the parking lot. If we had to pay the usual $200 an hour we couldn't afford it. A while back, the church roof sprang a leak. The following Saturday a dozen men were up there patching it. All of our organists, cantors, catechists, and church cleaners are volunteers (Yes, even in these days when more and more people are working and there aren't as many volunteers). The money we don't spend on these and many other items is a great source of saving that enables us to send people away to workshops and to help out others.

We don't have a budget. This might not be wise for a more complex parish, but we're not that large at 920 families. With no school and a comparatively tiny staff we don't have to be that elaborate and work on some annual budget. If the money's there, fine. If not, we'll wait till another time. But, as I said before, we trust the people will spend carefully for their needs and that no imbalance of priorities will take place. Our parish council helps us here.

The final factor in "How do you do it, pay for it?" is the tender issue of leadership. The quality of leadership is critical. The leader not only inspires vision, but he or she must work with the people as well as for them. People are anxious that the pastor relaxes and enjoys life and gets his vacation, but they cringe at any high living, absenteeism, designer labels, or materialism that underline his prophetic stance. They'll be less inclined to volunteer their time or talent or money to the man who can do it all by himself, who always asks for money (remember, "spirituality" was the first national yearning, not buildings or programs), or who can handsomely buy whatever he wants or thinks is good for the people.

"How do you do it?" I'm not really sure or that in these pages I've given an adequate answer. The people for whom I work and who pay my salary probably have better answers.

PART THREE

Hands Off

CHAPTER 16

Hands Off
the Hands-On

These days, and even more in the future, those putting the hands on the "hands-on" parish will be lay people. Why? Because of the growth of priestless parishes. One out of twenty parishes in our country is without a priest. By the year 2000, the already relatively small number of priests will be reduced 40 percent. It's worse elsewhere. More than 65 percent of the church worldwide does not have ordained priests. At least currently we have one priest for every 1000 Catholics, but in the Third World there is one priest for every 40,000 Catholics.[1] Vatican statistics show that of 368,000 parishes in the world, 157,000 have no resident priest. Add to this the increasing age of the clergy and the resultant loss through retirement, death, and, don't forget, resignation. In 1987, the diocese of

Seattle lost 18 priests and gained only two through new ordinations. In Chicago almost half of those ordained since 1976 have resigned. Since 1965, anywhere from 12,000 to 17,000 American priests have resigned and 86 percent of these were 45 years old or younger.[2] About 9800 priests in France and 5000 in Brazil have resigned. By 1990, the English dioceses of Westminster and Liverpool will have lost a quarter of the clergy. So it is around the world.

Also, what's coming up is down. Since 1966, the number of seminarians in the United States has fallen by four-fifths. In 1966-67, there were some 42,900 seminarians; in 1976-77, 18,300; in 1985-86, 10,800; in 1986-87, 10,400; in 1987-88, 9400, and in 1988-89, 9900. That's simply a devastating drop and it means that for many, many decades to come there will be an acute shortage of ordained priests everywhere (and where numbers are up, these men are needed where they are; not too many can be imported culturally or linguistically). Just to keep up with the status quo, dioceses in the United States would have to ordain 2,200 men a year for the next century or so. And the Catholic population is growing. If you want to sense the magnitude of the problem, translate all those figures into teachers or doctors and you can see what the crisis is. Most people still haven't felt the priest shortage directly, so it's often a case of out of sight, out of mind. But give it time.

Everyone is grappling with the problem. Pope John Paul II says that the crisis is a way of bringing us to our knees and he may be right:

> Today there are those who interpret the decline in priestly vocations since the council as a sign that the ministerial priesthood is to be superceded or greatly diminished, rather than complemented by new forms of ministry. Others argue that the requirement of celibacy for all Latin-rite priests should be abolished; still others claim that traditional doctrine about the priesthood, which is rooted in the institution of the sacrament by Christ and in Christian theology, should be abandoned, as if this were possible, so that women could be ordained to the priest-

hood. In these ways, it is asserted or implied, an abundance of laborers will be assured for the Lord's harvest.

May we not rather say that in keeping with God's ways and not our own, the ordained priesthood and the church's love and understanding of it are being tested, precisely so that what is essential may be strengthened, purified, and renewed in a spiritual rebirth to greater fruitfulness? If we are being brought to our knees, so to speak, by the need for more priests, is it not in order that we may understand with greater humility and love who the Lord of the harvest truly is?[3]

Bishops are going out of their minds wondering who's going to do the parish leadership job. Others see the crisis as basically an institutional problem, not a spiritual one; that is, the institutional church *could* ordain lots of others if it wanted to—married men, for instance—but as long as it insists on the discipline (not divine mandate) of the male celibate as the only candidate, the problem remains.

To fill the gap, bishops have resorted to closing or combining parishes and, more significantly perhaps, they have adopted a temporary solution, one that is quite effective in the short range but one, I believe, that will cause an intolerable tension and force a stand-off in the long run. The solution is twofold (1) the nonordained Pastoral Administrator, the man or woman in charge of the parish in everything except giving the sacraments, and (2) more lay involvement, people doing what was formerly the preserve of the clergy and religious. As to the latter, there are complaints that we are clericalizing the laity, making them priests without portfolio and underminding their in-the-world, properly secular task and witness. My own feeling is that, on the contrary, we are returning to the laity what was theirs all along. It is the institutional church itself that has clericalized nearly all the ministries that in fact originally and rightfully belonged to the laity. Just keep in mind my previous warning: all ministries, clerical or lay, are in service to the People of God.

The pastoral administrator, layman or laywoman, deacon or sister is operating right now in 70 of the nation's 167 dioceses. We might also note that as of 1988, women serve as chancellors in 17 dioceses and 82 women administer priestless parishes in 38 dioceses. Women also hold the position of diocesan superintendent of schools in 59 dioceses, 75 direct diocesan religious education programs, 39 direct family life offices, 28 edit diocesan newspapers or magazines, 26 head diocesan charities operations, 26 are directors of communications, 22 are marriage tribunal judges, and 20 serve as presidents of diocesan pastoral councils. But it's the parish administrator we're interested in here. There has been good acceptance of these leaders and they do a wonderful service. But the tension is growing. As such administrators move into people's lives, the disappointment grows when critical sacramental moments remain unfulfilled—for example, one who counsels another and listens to his or her confession but cannot give absolution; the people who faithfully bring the eucharist to the sick and prepare them for death but cannot anoint them; the one who does all the sacramental preparation and then must step aside; the one who leads the prayer service with imported hosts but cannot celebrate Mass. As one pastoral administrator from Chicago writes:

> I agree with the pastoral associates who say that it is hard to bring someone to a sacramental moment and then step aside. I find this to be true when I work with couples about to be married, with couples who've just had a baby, with people who are dying, and with the youth group when they experience God in community during a retreat, and come to the eucharist. Because of the team feeling that our staff has been able to establish, however, I don't resent this situation. In fact, I enjoy sharing the experience with others. I realize someday things will be different.[4]

But then there are the feelings and instincts of the people

who also realize that someday things will be different because they will want it so. For example, since there is the desire of a parish community to have a eucharistic spirituality, then naturally they would rather have a communion service with the pastoral administrator they know than to have a circuit priests they don't know pop in to celebrate a Mass. In short, more and more people are becoming, and will become, discontent with the sacraments not being connected to their immediate community life. As Peter Gilmour says:

"The more comfortable [the people] get with their community leader, the more they move in the direction of asking the question, 'Why can't our nonordained pastor celebrate the sacraments with us?'...The clerical system is OK as long as the priest is present. But when he's not present over a long period of time, people will begin to wonder why a virtually unknown 'holy man' must be called in to function at the climactic moment and then disappear. We can't go from a church of the eucharist to a church of the Word."[5]

Jean-Marie Hiesberger, director of the Institute for Pastoral Life in Kansas City, which teaches and upgrades ministers of all sorts, acknowledges that, given the priest shortage, questions "about our identity as a eucharistic church and questions abut the community's right to have the eucharist are going to become more prominent." One writer of a letter to the editor adds his voice:

If we as Roman Catholics do belong to a eucharistic community and if that eucharistic emphasis is one of the most striking distinguishing characteristics by which we are singled out from the other Christian communities, what does this say to us when the eucharistic celebration is becoming very different or possibly a rare occasion in many of our assemblies?[6]

Besides such common sense instincts of the people, there are good theological arguments against keeping the pastoral administrator or assistant apart from full sacramental powers. Read what Karl Rahner wrote on this whole issue in 1983:

> There is no point in upholding the theoretical principle that the ordained priest is and must remain the proper leader of the congregation if the increasing shortage of priests means that without laymen as leaders the congregations will cease to exist. If this schizophrenia is allowed to proliferate, the Church will be involved in a tacit Protestantization which it has hitherto so abhorred merely because of the desire (without convincing reasons) to continue to link the priesthood with an academic training and celibacy. Why, in fact? From the time of Pius X onward requirements for receiving Holy Communion have been reduced to a minimum, while requirements for presiding at the eucharistic celebration have been extended to what might be called a European maximum, which seems unreal, at least to the majority of people in the present day world. If leadership of the community is an intrinsic and essential element of the priesthood, in which this function and that of the presidency of the eucharistic celebration are mutually dependent, then the very people who in fact in the future will be leaders of a priestless community should themselves be ordained priests and thus sacramentally recognized for what they are and what they accomplish as actual leaders.
>
> ...if in practice, despite all sublime theological distinctions, the pastoral assistant in a priestless community exercises all the functions of a priestly community leader (apart from the two sacramental powers), we are faced with a dilemma. Either the functions actually undertaken by the pastoral assistant are regarded by no means specifically priestly. Then what is truly priestly about the ministerial priest is reduced to the two sacramental powers reserved to him alone; the priest becomes a purely cultic functionary. It has been said often enough that this inter-

pretation of priesthood is no longer acceptable today...Or
it is admitted that the functions actually undertaken by
the pastoral assistant are at bottom specifically priestly...

...If in practice the leadership of the community is en-
trusted to pastoral assistants and this commissioning can
be distinguished from a priest's community leadership
only by subtle theories; if in a modern theology of priesthood the two sacramental powers [confession and eu-
charist] reserved to ordained priests are basically articula-
tions and extrapolations of the priest's fundamental task
as leader of a local church and official representative of
the episcopal major church and of the church as a whole,
by what right are these two powers denied to the pastoral
assistant as community leader in a priestless community?
If someone as pastoral assistant is in fact appointed community leader, he is granted in this capacity the basic nature of the priest and at the same time refused the sacramental powers that flow from this basic nature. Is this
theologically consistent?[7]

I would say it is not consistent and that, therefore, the institutional church ought to relax its demands that each and every
leader must go through the full seminary training in order to
be ordained. In certain circumstances, there should be room
for life experience, charism, and proven de facto parish leadership as criteria for ordination. And ordination is important as
over against "appointment" or "being in charge." A study by
Hartford Seminary's Center for Social and Religious Research
has found that churchgoers *prefer* to be led by an ordained cleric rather than by a lay professional. Furthermore, about 60 percent of lay leaders from some 200 parishes in Catholic, Episcopal, Lutheran Church in America, and United Methodist
churches agreed that their congregations' morale would decline if they couldn't find full-time ordained leadership. So
what's that saying to us except, once more, ordination is important, too important to be confined to the rigid (and merely)

300-year-old seminary system. While we don't have to return to that civil magistrate, St. Ambrose, who was sent to quell a riot in the Milanese cathedral over the election of their new bishop and wound up being that bishop by popular acclamation, nevertheless, we should hold this "subversive memory" in mind. Another subversive memory:

> As we now watch the laity claim a greater role in the celebration of the sacraments, or witness the growing phenomenon of Sunday services celebrated without a priest, it is ironic to recall that priests themselves began to preside at eucharist only in response to a need for an increased number of celebrants. The fact that even to this day the ordination rite speaks of presbyters rather than of priests is a reminder of this.[8]

There are other practical considerations. Since the eucharist has been such a vital and critical part of Catholic tradition, it seems somehow disproportionate to trade off our eucharistic communities for a celibate clergy. I have a dilemma here, for I want to extol the value and witness of celibacy and indeed to pay respects to recent scholarship which indicates the apostolic origins of such celibacy as a part of simple gospel radicalism ("eunuchs for the sake of the Kingdom, Matthew 19:12).[9] Nor do I entertain those illusions which maintain that a married male clergy will make priests more effective or happier. On the contrary, there are no data to suggest that. The data in fact makes it clear that there is no significant difference between the psychological and psycho-sexual development of priests and other American males (Kennedy study; also Weisgerber, 1977). Moreover, the Survey of Young Catholics in 1980 indicated

> that the real obstacle for young people, male or female, in considering a vocation to religious life was simply that no one had ever suggested it to them or encouraged them at any time recently in considering that move. Celibacy was

indeed a factor, but only during the late stages of decision-making.... For the last few years, celibacy has actually been coming back into vogue in the popular culture, partially due to a seriously flawed sexual revolution, and more recently, to the risks associated with promiscuous sexual behavior.[10]

The dilemma concerns a clash of values: the eucharist or celibacy. The feelings of the people, who surely must prize celibacy, showed that 73 percent favored married priests (Gallup). This not voting in faith and morals by majority rule, but it is stressing the ability of people to move a man-made discipline around to preserve a higher gospel value. Opening up the priesthood to the married widens the opportunity for us to hold dearly to the "Mass That Matters." What's more, it's been done. We do have a pretty good tradition going for us. For the first ten centuries, celibacy was never a *condition* for ordination (though it was seen as an ideal, perhaps back to the apostles themselves) and there is no theological support whatsoever for such a condition. Still, there are problems and Archbishop Pilarczyk of Cincinnati sums them up nicely:

> Changing the church's policy of ordaining only celebrates to priesthood could bring with it as many problems as it proposes to solve. These problems include those of financial support, of mobility, of numbers, of marriage strain and divorce, of tension between married and celibate priests. What effects would come from the necessary sense of loss which parishioners would feel as they learn that the priest is no longer "theirs" in the same way he was before? What implications about the church's teaching on human sexuality, about matrimony, and, indeed, about the nature of priesthood itself lie hidden in such a change?

On the other hand, the Pro-Nuncio to Great Britain, Archbishop L. Barbarito, at the meeting of the National Conference of Priests, said that the main measure envisioned, if the celibate priest shortage should continue, would be the ordination of married men. This would be necessary, he added, "if it were the only way to insure availability of the sacraments." (His opinion is that priests who are already married will never be readmitted.) At least he expresses our pastoral dilemma. You might add to his voice that of a French bishop, Bishop Gaillot who, citing that the number of priests in France will drop to half its 1950 level in the next ten years, has called for a married clergy. He also noted that most of the priests who have left in the past 20 years did so because they wanted to be married, yet still went on to work for the church in one way or another. We might note also that the Canon Law Society of America has on its agenda a working paper concerning the ordination of married men. We have here, as you can see, more and more "official" voices raising the issue.

Again, the key issue to me is the issue of the sacraments. I understand that a major Vatican worry is that the church in Latin America, with its shortage of priests and its Scripture sharing, lay-led base communities, is fast becoming a non-sacramental church. This fear is well founded. It is reminiscent of the days when the Jesuits were suppressed in Mexico and who, before they left, taught the natives to baptize, and to celebrate a "dry" Mass. Eventually, this kind of ministry supplanted that of the ordained clergy, and in time the people came to see no reason for anything else. They grew up without a sacramental spirituality. That's the danger for all of Latin America and eventually Asia and our own country.

Beneath all of these practical considerations lies a critical theoretical one. It has to do with the nature of the eucharist itself. The proper triad is Sunday + Assembly + Eucharist. It's an integral package. That is, what makes the Mass the Mass is that the whole worshiping assembly *together* prays the Eucharistic Prayer, shouts "Amen" at its end, and proceeds to share the sacred Bread and Cup—those very same elements over which hands were extended, those very elements that are but a part of the overall eucharistic celebration. It's all one movement, one act of communal worship.

However, with the introduction of the communion service (even the official one from Rome issued in the fall of 1988) you have now made a distinction, an unnatural separation, between the eucharist and holy communion, between the active sacramental celebration of the whole people and the passive reception of a "by-product." That is to say, you separate communion from the larger pattern of the eucharist, from the whole organic worship of the assembly; you isolate one particular item and build a service around it. You say in effect that the eucharistic prayer is irrelevant to the assembly and irrelevant to communion itself. It is merely a long wind-up to get to the "real point." On the contrary, the sacramental celebration of the Lord's death and resurrection, the celebration of the paschal mystery, *is* the essence of the Mass. Once you allow an artificial ceremony, such as a communion service, then the whole body of Christ is simply *not* celebrating the eucharistic paschal mystery. Rather, it is gathering for the ecclesiastical "bottom line": to receive communion.

A holy communion community is not a eucharistic community, no matter how many prayers and songs surround it. A people who have come together for the loveliest of communion services is not a people who have celebrated the passion, death, and resurrection of Jesus. You see the point? You see what is happening from the theological point of view? We are winding up, not with a Sunday without priests. We are winding up with a Sunday without eucharist! We are winding up underscoring the impotence and passivity of the worshiping community, the very thing we have been trying so hard to undo. Yes, that communion service comes along and effectively tells the people that they, the assembly, no longer celebrate as they were taught by Vatican II. No, someone else far away celebrates by himself or with another assembly and this community waits to receive the end product concerning which they had no active part. In the long run, it is this sort of arrangement that may do more harm than good to the People of God. Surely, then, it is infinitely better to consider widening the criteria for ordination than to allow the People of God communion while depriving them to the eucharist, to allow them the species while depriving them of the celebration, to allow them the devotion while depriving them of full participation and worship.

Meanwhile, what other course is open? One, I suppose, is that the church could allow pastoral administrators to administer the sacraments by special indult: baptism and even the sacrament of the sick and reconciliation. But then that adds to the already fractured identity of the priest (not to mention the deacon). Then we're back to the problem: the danger of becoming a non-sacramental church, a kind of Catholic congregationalism.

And there's still the emotional and practical problems. I myself would not like to be on the negative end of the separation of pastoral and sacramental ministry—all that service, all that nearness to the sacramental realities, and not to be able to follow through! All that readiness standing at the altar, and year after year waiting for the hosts to arrive (Jesus via UPS as some wag has said), and no power to complete the connection, so to speak! (I read somewhere that a priest, the only one in a distant rural parish, was staying in Rome for three months to attend a synod. Someone asked him, "And who's minding the store, Father?" He replied, "Oh, everything's fine. I consecrated 4000 hosts before I left.") Nor, as a diocesan priest, would I like to be a circuit rider. I'm not an order priest living in community. The parish is my community, my family, and just to "visit" different ones now and then would destroy my sense of being as leader of *this* community.

And so, inspired by Rahner's ideas, I make a suggestion: Why not go back to the old rule from the fifth-century Council of Chalcedon (Canon 6) that forbade someone to be ordained a free-floating priest at large, that is, without a community? (That abuse gave rise to a sense of personal power, not community service.) Then, on the other hand, ordain someone (namely the pastoral administrator) *from* this particular community and *for* this community. Then put a time restriction on this, say, for seven or ten years. The idea behind this (compromise) approach is this: perhaps a man (if they want to stick with a man), a celibate or widower, could be ordained for this community as its presider. After the seven to ten years he would have the option of renewing his commitment or else be relieved of the presider's job and the discipline and promise of celibacy and go on to another life. He could still be a "priest forever," but his jurisdiction would be confined (as is common in many instances today) to being "weekend help" for that same community, even as a married man. This gets in-between: the institutional church gets its celibate male, the community gets its legitimate presider, the man himself gets a chance, if he wishes, to marry, and the church gets to preserve its ideal of celibacy through the symbol of allowing him only weekend work once he is married. Taken for granted is that such a pastoral administrator will not have to undergo that long full-time seminary training now required for seminarians. Rather, he can have the same kind of course that married deacons have, a few nights a week over the course of two or three years.

I realize that this notion of a kind of "temporary priesthood" may, as someone has pointed out, weaken the marriage bond in the eyes of the people. People do tend to equate the "priest forever" with marriage vows: if you can break one, you can break the other. They do not distinguish between church-made and God-made law. Theologically, being a "priest forever" need not mean functioning that way forever. History is full of hyphenated priests whose work brought them completely out of the sanctuary. Jurisdiction has always limited the priest's right to function as a priest, as have legitimate laicization processes. So the church has a lot of spatial and temporal flexibility here, whereas the law of the indissolubility of marriage comes from God. Still, in one way or another, a matter of rights is involved and that's the tension: namely, the right of the People of God to "do this in remembrance of me." Such a right supersedes any moveable discipline. That right is so grounded, so traditional, so "Catholic" that I can foresee what will happen. What will happen is that gradually a pastoral administrator and a community will reach such a point of tension, of longing, of intolerable deprivation, that the pastoral administrator will celebrate the eucharist. Some bishops will instantly discipline this, but somewhere, someday, one bishop, out of concern for his people, will look the other way and the gates will crack open. Even last year at a large gathering of lay and religious hospital chaplains, the question was asked how many anoint the sick and, to the sound of nervous laughter, almost all hands went up. So with the eucharist. Some are already celebrating it. I don't agree with this because that celebration is individual and personal and not related to the unity of all the churches symbolized by the eucharist and official ordination. But on the other hand, is there a greater reality here?

> The group must ritualize its specific way of following Christ before it can ritualize its unity with others. An outsider who "has faculties, will preside" is as close to the shepherd hireling Jesus talks about in the Gospel of John as we are likely to find. Such a presider can only symbolize the abstract unity of all the local groups, not the concrete reality over whose ritual he is presiding. At best, this is incomplete; at worst, ritually ineffective.[11]

In any case, a friendly Lutheran minister asks, What, even in the spirit of ecumenism, should Catholics, "under no circumstances, negotiate"?:

> It may be surprising to Catholic readers, but as a Protestant with 25 years experience in ecumenical work, I find there are some elements of Catholic faith and practice that should never be surrendered. The first of these is the centrality of the Mass....Another very important element is the role of the clergy. Most Catholics still have a strong respect for the priest as God's ordained representative, charged with the spiritual and temporal leadership of a parish....The Catholic emphasis on the priest as leader of the Christian community needs to be reinforced if the continuity of the Church is to be realized.[12]

Well, it's been a long chapter, but bear with me for one final thought. Let's go back to the other solution to the priest short-age, closing or consolidating parishes. As for closing parishes, one bishop, Raymond Lucker of Minnesota, lets the people de-cide if parishes should close, and there's no need to if they're viable—viable being defined as having at least 100 families and an annual operating income of $50,000.[13] Not bad criteria: decision by the people and financial viability. It's worth adopt-ing. As for consolidation, there's no doubt that some long over-the-hill parishes should be consolidated with more vigor-ous ones and that parish programs should be regionalized (clustered) and duplication done away with. Still, to consoli-date into too large a parish, strictly as an alternative to the priest shortage, again defeats community. People naturally prefer small parish communities. We all do. Pius X thought the ideal number of families per parish is 100. I wonder what he would think of parishes with 3000 to 7000 families? The parish is really important and incredibly serviceable in our United States. It has always been so, and the people love it. It remains what I once called "the basic ward unit of the church politic," the backbone of the people's religious life. If all this is true, then we're back to a real dilemma: consolidating parishes, while helpful, might pull too many of them into megaparishes. Community will suffer. Clergy will suffer. Priests or the parish director will get frustrated as they wind up being distant man-agers of all the staff needed in such large places. That report on priests from the Bishops' Committee on Priestly Life and Min-istry realistically commented on the burden of heavier work-loads, "long and painful battles over consolidation and closure of parishes, and less probability of retirement at all." Levels of intermediaries, helpers, volunteers, etc. are helpful, but close-ness still takes a beating. One of the appeals of fundamentalist congregations is the caring, warm community that knows you by name. The priest or pastoral administrator in large consoli-dated parishes can only know a portion of the persons in their area of work. Once more, then, the needs of a viable communi-ty and the needs of the pastor, like the need to celebrate the eu-charist, cry out for another solution to the shortage than mere closing and consolidation. As attractive as closing and consolidation may be under the circumstances, they are still self-defeating both to community building and to dealing with the real issues.

❑ About ten years ago, seeing the shortage of priests becoming more acute and wishing to prepare my own community for the possibility of a priestless parish, I began discussing changing the weekly liturgical format. We had Mass daily except on Saturdays (weddings plus evening Masses made that absence practical). I suggested that since there are three official liturgical ways of worship, Mass, sacraments, and the divine office, we might want to try the last as a substitute on Thursday mornings. We got the *Catholic Worship Book* and used that. We tried it for a while, with me leading the prayer. The people learned quickly and voted to continue, and then gradually they began to lead the office themselves—including the hymns, Scripture reading, and homily. Now for years it has been entrenched, and many people are quite comfortable in leading public worship. Later we substituted a prayer service on Monday mornings with the same result. We consolidated the two Saturday evening Masses into one when we lost a weekend helper and could get no replacement. Having the people lead the Stations of the Cross during Lent, gathering in Bible study and Renew groups, having Lay Witness Sunday, and the public Divine Office (as well as three times a week at 6:30 A.M. before all dash off to work) again has geared the people to lead worship and prayer and to expect it.

Some might see all this as self-defeating, like consolidating viable parishes. Why make people content with this kind of substitution and keep their attention from the real problem, a problem moreover that in fact has a solution at hand: ordain more people, people beyond the standard male celibate? The answer is that, given the current climate, you do second best while keeping the ideal of first best alive.

As the title of this chapter suggests, the new reality is that many hands are part of the "hands-on" parish, and many of those hands must keep hands off. So, to put it mildly, fuzziness, traffic, and tension have arisen and are not going to be easily resolved. Look at this scenario: you have a pastor, a pastoral assistant, a deacon, religious and active laity all in one diocese. The pastor, ordained and empowered, may be a sacramental circuit rider with no community. The pastoral assistant is the actual appointed community leader but is not ordained and so lacks important powers (absolution and consecration). The deacon is ordained, but also lacks these two powers. The religious and laity give expertise and are paid or are volunteers. So, the pastor has the powers but no practical community. The pastoral administrator, deacon, and laity have community, but not the priestly powers. That adds up to a lot of tension and frustration, and should at least be openly acknowledged. It seems to me, therefore, that at the very least the current situation demands a lot of training together.[13] That is, seminarians should be taught the dynamics of cooperation and sharing and relating to pastoral administrators who are their equals as community leaders. The pastoral administrators and laity in general should have forums and mechanisms to deal with tensions. And all should pressure for better, more realistic, solutions. And we know what they are: reasonably small faith communities with their own ordained community leaders, that is, their own priests. What's more, we know these leaders are there. There's no shortage of them. They only await ordination.

CHAPTER 17

Pastoral
Reflections

In this chapter I just want to express some random thoughts and opinions (not especially enlightened); a kind of "Oh, by the way, I think this is important." Whether anyone else does is another matter. But for what it's worth, here are a few things I'm thinking of these days:

Prayer Rhythms

[Younger Catholics] are concerned about religion in their own lives. Most of them feel that their parishes are not dealing with their interest in religion in general, and their spiritual growth and sustenance in particular. If a parish is successful in dealing with these matters, that parish is regarded as successful...What the younger Catholics are looking for is a more spiritual response from the church, and they want that at an individual level. The parish is set up to respond more to the community than to the individual. But the spiritual need is experienced at the latter level.[1]

Thus says sociologist William McCready. Never mind for the moment what we have observed before, that they are preoccupied with their own lives at the expense of social consciousness. Note the positive: the desire and need for spirituality.

That means that woven throughout parish life must be the strands of prayer. This is not just a pious observation, but a hard reality. If the prophet says that without vision the people perish, so without prayer the parish perishes. Beyond the regular and expected weekend and daily liturgies—and homilies that openly deal with matters of spirituality— and sacraments, the people of the parish (the people who *are* the parish) must have a sense of what they're about and why. Education for the head is one way we have mentioned. Equally important is "education" for the spirit. In addition to the presence and symbol of a full-time parish spiritual director mentioned in a previous chapter, there are other spiritual rhythms that mark out intent.

Three times a week, for example, at 6:30 A.M. (It's challenging on those dark winter days) we gather to chant morning prayer in our spiritual center chapel. The men come two mornings a week and the women one. (The men started it about eight years ago and as the numbers grew, split into two groups. The women followed a few years later.) It's a marvelously prayerful time with each of us taking turns leading. It's a general way to begin the day—to publicly pray with one's parishioners.

❑ Moreover, by personal invitation I invite eight men once a month to come with me to a little log cabin I have (in a simple row-house neighborhood, not, alas, in the splendid isolation by some lake) for an evening of reflection from 8:00 to 10:00. I keep strictly to the time as a reassurance to them. We start with a prayer and hymn, usually see a half-hour video (one of

Vincent Dwyer's tapes, for instance) and then have a reflection and sharing, time for quiet prayer, and a closing prayer and hymn. I make a point here of stressing that these evenings are for the men because the women always seem to have many opportunities (and perhaps more inclination) for prayer and retreats. The men always seem to me to be neglected. Perhaps that is why, among other reasons, there are so many women who are really the backbone of our parishes. The men just give the money, but it is the women who give the time and work, thus exploding the myth that it takes males to run an organization. Perhaps parishes contribute to that myth by their hesitancy to tap the spiritual power of men. Richard Rohr has addressed the issue well.[2] He speaks of "converting" men to the feminine and women to the masculine in a kind of Christian yin and yang balance. "A masculine spirituality would be one that encourages men to take the radical gospel journey from their unique beginning point, in their own unique style, with their own unique goals." Anyway, it's an unbalanced parish that does not find inventive ways for its men to contribute their balance of spirituality—and participation. And we know there's an imbalance when the current "in" joke refers to the church as an Officer's Club and the parish as a harem.

Each parish organization is required to have at least one day or evening of recollection a year, and several weekends are offered as well. During the hour the kids are at CCD, the spiritual director meets with the mothers to lead them in prayer and direction. Each CCD class itself, several times a year, puts aside a class (in church or chapel to change the atmosphere) for instruction in how to pray. Parish prayer groups, opportunities for spiritual direction, and a parish library filled mostly with books (and tapes) on the bible and spirituality add up to the statement of the necessity of prayer, both privately and as a community.

The Responsive Parish

Beyond the importance of prayer, there's another rhythm that marks a parish as alive and responsive. The difficult thing is that it's hard to pin down or put precisely, but the key is probably in the last word of the last sentence: responsive. I look at the growing power of the evangelical churches ranging from the moderate evangelical churches to the right-wing fundamentalist anti-Catholic agendas of the Bob Joneses and Jimmy Swaggarts. The scandals of some of their notorious leaders have not, in the least, dampened the allegiance of the faithful who still give time, talent, and money to the evangelical and fundamentalist causes. For all of the media hype and hullabaloo over the scandals, few have bothered with the essential questions: who are the congregations of such churches? What is the appeal? What chord are the evangelists striking and what do people find in them?

It is axiomatic that mainline liberal Protestantism is dying, and equally axiomatic that Catholicism seems divided as ever, but for those who can't wait until the dust settles and are sick to death over promiscuous sex, drugs, and rootlessness, the evangelicals at least provide consistent and appealing themes of traditional family values, temperance, and community sharing. In other words, such churches, whatever one thinks of them, are responsive—they respond to people's needs. Their preachers give straightforward and unambiguous sermons on loneliness, youth, family, and marriage. I'm not making judgments here on content, or politics, or theology, just on the dynamics that we would do well to attend to:

> Diane Castillo's 21-year marriage was on the rocks when she came forward on the first night of a Denver crusade in July 1987. "He talked about marriage, how the commitment one makes to God comes first and He loves you and forgives you for whatever you've done," she recalls. A former Roman Catholic, Castillo, 41, now regularly attends a Baptist church and enjoys a healed relationship with her husband, Richard, who had "accepted the Lord" three years ago.[3]

I guess I'm saying that both in its homily content and in its healing groups a parish has to address the real needs that appeal to and gather in (and reclaim) the Dianes of this land. I come again to the need for a parish to create that climate in which people feel free to assemble in whatever "community of communities" they desire and need. In fact, there are literally thousands upon thousands of groups that meet every week in America, from Narcotics Anonymous to Tough Love. Perhaps they represent an artificial regrouping of a country that has idolized individualism too much and found it intolerable. In any case, at the bottom of all these groups is an unspoken (and sometimes spoken) need for God by whatever name. I just read an article in *Newsweek* (December 1988) by a Benjamin Stein, whose novel thesis is that soon we'll hear some serious God-talk on television, based on the premise that whatever is on writers' minds will find its way into scripts. Well, in Los Angeles where he lives, there are 2000 AA meetings a week (not to mention Narcotics Anonymous, Gamblers Anonymous, or Cocaine Anonymous, etc.) peopled by actors, writers, and producers. They go to AA, which is "not unlike a revival meeting" where they are "being saved":

> ...all of these 12-step programs devote a lot of time and attention to praising God for lifting the curse of their addiction one day at a time. Fully six of the famous 12 steps of AA talk about relying on God or following a "Higher Power." AA, in short, is like a religion. And at the present moment, this religion is sweeping Hollywood.

Hence, in due time, Stein maintains, this consciousness is going to surface in television and movie scripts. I'm skeptical, but the point is the vast phenomenon of groups all over the country positions the parish to be receptive to them, to be a center for hospitality for them, or at least to encourage them. I think of the Catholic support groups for public school teachers in southern California, for lawyers and their spouses in San Francisco and Chicago, and the U.S. Senators who meet for weekly prayer and mutual support, hoping that, in the words of Senator Paul Simon, "we can accommodate our political actions to our religious beliefs rather than the other way around."

Hispanics

As a pastor and as an American, I cannot help but be conscious of the growing Hispanic presence in the country, as I also cannot help being conscious of how little we reach out to them. For one practical matter, very few lay ministry programs throughout the country (and many seminaries) require the learning of Spanish as a second language.

What are the facts? Between 1980 and 1987, Latinos have grown 30 percent in this country. Their population is expected to double in 30 years and triple in 60. There are some 19 million of them now, and in less than a dozen years there will be an estimated 30 million Hispanics. Moreover, the Hispanic community is predominantly young, with two in every five Latinos being under 20 years old, and only one in twenty being elderly. They have more poverty and unemployment than whites and blacks. The national fertility rate is 23 percent higher than the national average for all women, and among Hispanic teenagers it is 34 percent higher. Single mothers are more apparent in the Hispanic community than elsewhere.

> This growth will probably have a major effect on the Catholic Church in the United States...[Hispanics] do not see themselves as immigrants. Their roots were well sunk into our southern borders and coastlands before the Pilgrims ever set sail from Plymouth. They do not want to be assimilated, they wish to retain their culture and their language.[4]

That's important to remember: Hispanics are natives who wish to keep their culture and language, so it's not a question of changing them to us. It's a question of us accommodating to them. The evangelical Protestants see that very well. They are vigorous and well financed in their pursuit of the Hispanics.

This has been officially noted. In his address to the U.S.

Bishops, apostolic pronuncio Archbishop Iio Laghi said, "The annual loss of Spanish-speaking Catholics to non-Catholic sects is significantly—I would say disturbingly—high." He urges us to be not only bi-lingual but (more difficult) bicultural. And then he adds, significantly, "One reason why the sects appear attractive to some Hispanic Catholics—and not only to Hispanics either—concerns their unabashed preaching of Jesus Christ, the word of God as found in the Bible and a clear, appealing moral code." I wonder if those three items might not be a focus for a day's reflection among staff and personnel.

Alternate Parishes

I am a true believer in the parish and its durability and usefulness. Nevertheless, I want to say boldly that its current structure need not apply everywhere. I mean that the parish reflects the Vatican in miniature with its chain of command and schedule and priorities. No problem here. But does it have to be this way all over? Hispanics, for example, prefer a less structured "plant," one more charismatic, more communal, more in keeping with base communities. Need we have a rectory or even a church building? Could there not be a more vigorous devotional life, heavier biblical emphasis and family-centered activities? Could not preaching be more in focus? Could we not have more missions, cursillos, and a more free-floating clergy who specialize in teaching and preaching?

We are so used to the parish structure as we know it—a pastor doing ministry in union with the bishop, and a stable community of faith—that we think it was that way for all times. Yet history shows that, especially from the thirteenth century on, many religious ministries arise *not* from the parish structure or from office, but from the needs of the people. The thirteenth-century Dominicans and Franciscans for example, although very much "in union with Rome," operated very much with a different spirituality and process, ministering more from charism than from office. Their ministry was in fact exempt from the supervision of the episcopacy. Theirs (and other religious orders) was what is called a "ministry of interiority" and they made retreats, preaching, missions, conducting schools, and running hospitals and orphanages into legitimate forms of ministry. To this extent, such orders reflected the charismatic, wandering ministrations of, say, a St. Paul, rather than the stable parish-congregation of Matthew or the stable congregations that an Ambrose or Augustine knew. We must remember that for many centuries when people thought of the "church" they did not think of the parish but of the itinerant preachers or religious orders and their centers. Furthermore, it is instructive to remember that at the Middle Ages most influential ecumenical council, the Fourth Lateran Council of 1215, there were 400 bishops present, but 800 abbots.

What I'm saying is that in our long tradition ministry was not always structured

> with an eye to a local and stable community as symbolized by the parish, but transcended diocese and even nation—"to go anywhere in the world," as the Jesuit Constitutions says....Even among the faithful, religious orders and congregations have tended to have a special interest in those whom the ordinary ministry of the Church for one reason or another failed to reach: orphans, young vagrants, prostitutes, the "alienated"—or, on the other hand, those laity seeking to devote themselves to God and their neighborhood beyond the rhythms of word and sacrament in more challenging and unconventional ways.[5]

This is true. Think, for example, of what you tell the person who wants to do "more" for God and the church. You don't send him or her to join the Rosary Altar society or become a lector. You give that person the name and address of the Jesuit Volunteer Center or some such and off they go to Tanzania or the inner city.

Do you see what I'm saying? The parish-hierarchial, word-sacrament structure, as good as it is, is not the only viable structure in our history, not by a long shot. Other styles, from the twelfth and thirteenth centuries on, have been used with great effect. We of the parish institution absolutely need the charisms of the religious orders and lay institutes. I know the relationship hasn't always been balanced, to say the least, but the alliance is necessary.

In one of my more fervent pastoral fantasies, I am "pope for a day." If I were "pope for a day," I would pronounce a policy of ratio; that is, for every twenty parishes I would mandate a spiritual center, a retreat house, a learning center—you name it—that would work closely with the twenty parishes, be partially financed by them, and whose sole purpose would be to catch the between-the-cracks that no parish, by definition and structure, can possibly handle. The reality is that our parish structure almost precludes getting to "the orphans, young vagrants, prostitutes, the alienated," the latchkey kids, the young adults, unwed mothers and drop-outs. Nor can we offer a variety of "spiritualities." We need an "adjunct." And in an ideal world these twenty parishes and spiritual centers would work in close cooperation. If I were a bishop I would work hard to work out some arrangement like this, if for no other reason than that our tradition is full of its successes; and if for no other reason than such "special" missions and ministries, such a variety of charisms, are needed more than ever today:

> The division of labor is not an accident of history. It reflects the two traditions that over the course of the centuries have manifested themselves with uneven beat but with considerable consistency in ways that can only be suggested here. The vocabulary, for instance, is different. On the one hand, words like "office" and "parish" recur, while on the other we find "need" and "mission." "Hierarchy" predominates in one, whereas "fraternity" or its equivalent is found in the other. For the one, "apostolic" indicates a conduit of authority; for the other, it suggests a style of life and ministry. For the first, ministry seems modeled on the Pastoral Epistles, the letters of Ignatius of

Antioch, and the examples of Ambrose and Augustine. For the second, it seems modeled on Jesus and his disciples in the Synoptics, the itinerant Paul of his letters and Acts, and the example of the charismatic layman (later deacon), Francis. In the one instance, the model of Church as sacrament seems especially operative; in the other, the Church as herald. The former relates more easily to "priest"—celebrant for the community and its public servant; the latter more easily to "prophet"—spokesperson and agent for special points of view.[6]

That makes good pastoral sense in my opinion, and even more so if, for example, you wanted to apply this to the Hispanic issue mentioned above.

Authority

The issue of authority in the local church is also one that we have to reflect on. It's far from resolved and probably won't be for a long time. All we can do here is raise the issue. You see, the issue has become more pressing as so many laity participate in parish life and function as volunteers and professionals or pastoral administrators. Besides that, the laity is generally well-educated and they hold a very strong "American" mentality. So the questions are: Can Father still rule the parish? Can lay participation in decision making remain token? Can the wide gap between official pronouncements and the actual experience of people ministering go unnoticed and unarticulated? People know that in the old hierarchical system, born in the Middle Ages, you *couldn't* have a parish community without the priest. They also know that in the Revised Code of Canon Law, you *can* have a parish community without the priest. He can come and go. They stay. So, in such a context, what are the mechanisms for sharing in decision making? This doesn't have to imply rule by majority or consensus. It just implies something more than the solo, temporary, clerical performer who makes the solitary and irrevocable pronouncements on behalf of the stable community.[7]

Fundamentalism

This last issue that I think should be addressed is one that is a growing challenge for the church. I gave a course on fundamentalism last year and the research on it showed me what an extraordinary challenge it is. Up until 15 or 20 years ago, no Catholic ever heard Protestant preaching. Now there are some 65 television stations and 168 radio stations broadcasting evangelicalism, and they are very effective in converting Catholics and mainstream Protestants. Furthermore, this exposure to evangelicalism is made easier not only by the official ecumenical openness but by the simple fact that many Catholics have now moved to the Bible Belt, have Protestant neighbors, and suddenly find themselves going to Bible study classes with them. Moreover, the certainties that were once the stock trade of Catholics have been lost—what two Catholics, official or otherwise, agree on anything? Many Catholics find themselves falling into line behind the fundamentalists who, with vigor and confidence, preach what saves—and *who* saves. Their personal relationship with Jesus is an appealing hallmark. Their literal Bible reading, with a text for every ache and pain, cuts across the endless distinctions and subtleties of mainline religions that still argue about Jesus' divinity and deny any physical resurrection, but maintain instead that the point of Easter is that Jesus is now above to be with everybody in a new way. They remind me that history seems to credit the incredible success of Mohammed to a cry that cut right through the endless and scandalous wranglings among the Christians about the Trinity. "There is only One God, Allah, and Mohammed is his prophet!" That, at least, was neat and understandable. Fundamentalists are neat and understandable. Their absolute sense of American moral and family values and their justly famed hospitality and small, caring congregations stand out in contrast to some Catholic parishes that embrace "alternate lifestyles" and are so huge as to defy any sense of community.

There are some excellent and insightful official papers on fundamentalism that have been issued by the secretariats of the Holy See and our United States Bishops' Conference. Three worth noting are: "Challenges to New Religious Movements" (May 1986, Holy See); "Proselytism Among Today's Immigrants: A Preliminary Report" (U.S.C.C., February 1987), and "A Pastoral Statement for Catholics on Biblical Fundamentalism" (N.C.C.B., March 1986). These documents are very informative, straightforward, and honest. In general, they highlight the points we made above, namely: Fundamentalism's personalism and community, its smallness and hospitality, its unabashedly affective or emotive approach and, significantly, the fact that these sects or small congregations *have ministers who come from the people themselves.* The official acknowledgment of this, in the light of what we have written in Chapter 15, should make us ponder all over again the priest shortage we are experiencing.

Let me share a striking case of fundamentalism's appeal and approach. It is reported (*The Catholic Register*, January 15, 1989) that one of the largest and fastest growing Christian churches in the nation attracts 5000 to 6000 former Catholics every weekend among its 12,000 weekly attendants, and has been converting 400 to 500 Catholics each year. It's the Willow Creek Community Church in South Barrington, a Chicago suburb. It took some courage, but the Archdiocese of Chicago invited the pastor, Bill Hybels, to speak to them about evangelization. Hybels estimates that 40 to 50 percent—and perhaps more—of his churchgoers are former Catholics. Hybels said he did his "market" research first and asked people why they didn't attend church. The answers in order of frequency were (1) they're always asking for money; (2) I don't like the music; (3) I can't relate to the message; (4) it doesn't meet my needs; (5) the services are predictable and boring; and (6) they make me feel guilty.

He tried to respond to those needs by taking an approach that is novel and imitable. First, he says, because most people are highly insulated from any kind of Christianity in society, it is important that someone who is a believer build a relationship with them. Second, sooner or later such believers must give actual verbal witness to these people. Third, they should invite them to a Sunday service. Fourth, then invite them to the more in-depth Wednesday night services. Fifth, get them into small groups (our "storytelling" groups) for Bible reading and friendship. Six, get them involved in ministry, and finally, get them in turn to go out and recruit others.

But I was more interested in what else he does—something I've mentioned in Chapter 14. Hybels is very methodical in instructing the people at Sunday service. He knows in his heart what we know: people, even the otherwise educated, are religious beginners and they need evangelization. He teaches the fundamentals of the faith. He uses dramatic skits and he uses professional actors. He makes it alive, and spends 20 to 30 hours a week on his sermons. He shapes Sunday services for beginners and has the Wednesday nights for the more advanced. The teaching is unambiguous, clear, professional. Commenting on this, Chicago's Father Patrick Brennan, the head of Catholic evangelization, notes an interesting contrast: "I know somebody who has a friend taking instruction in the Catholic faith, and already she's been given three different opinions on birth control." He is also honest enough to comment about the Willow Creek Community, "Many folks dismiss them, saying 'All the Catholics that go over there, they'll eventually come back.' But I've known none who've come back."

Can we learn something from Reverend Hybels, who attracts 12,000 people to worship each week? Couldn't we have a longer Mass with a longer Liturgy of the Word, yes, even with professional skits? Could we not give a well-tuned series? Yes and no are the answers, of course. We protest loudly that we dare not—and perhaps cannot (remember the chapter on the Covenant)—make demands on our people. They wouldn't stand for being in church more than 50 minutes. (Why, think of the parking lot!) But why not? Couldn't at least one Mass a month be advertised as a special learning Mass with a well-rounded series that would take about an hour and a half, maybe two hours? Could we not do something with Wednesday nights ourselves? Couldn't the diocese hire some real pros to go around giving a great series at Masses? After all, all those fundamentalists and evangelicals get the people out several times every week—and that includes all those Catholics who we said wouldn't come out. It is a fact that our number of converts has declined. It is time to take a survey, to "market" the problem and the needs, and then to invest lots of money into the talents and training of clergy and laity who, knowing we have indeed a marvelous message and tradition, are skilled in getting both across.[8]

❑ Here's an idea. I'm not sure it's valid, but I'd like to propose a pastoral variation taken from the R.C.I.A. process. As you know, it is permitted and encouraged for those catechizing the R.C.I.A. candidates to leave Mass right after the liturgy of the Word and go off with them for the instruction. Such people are automatically excused from the obligation of attending Mass. So here's my idea. Why couldn't we apply this concept to the whole parish? Inasmuch as so many really need evangelization (yes, even our best and most educated are socially and by public policy "insulated from any kind of Christianity"), why couldn't we take, let's say, three or four or six weeks and *in place of Mass*, show a good video series or have a superior teaching series of speakers for the hour? It would be understood that this is temporary, but if the concerns of the R.C.I.A. make this attractive for candidates, why not for the whole parish? My guess is that we would get a very positive reaction and reception. The series could even be tracked for different age levels such as we do now when we have the children leave for their own liturgy of the Word. It could even be featured as a yearly event, eventually a part of parish life and rhythm.

Anyway, I recall that years ago the Brooklyn diocese closed down all its parishes one weekend to dramatize the shortage of priests. If people can be excused for that reason, then they surely can be excused for the process of their own re-learning and re-conversion. As a pastor I am excited about this prospect, since I am convinced that we desperately need evangelization, as I am convinced that the weekends are, as always, the best and most efficient and effective opportunities to regroup our people once more around who and what we are as disciples of Christ. I can only hope that some bishops would see the possibilities here and give them their official blessing.

The fundamentalists are making great inroads especially, as we have seen, among the Hispanics. All in all, there should be a much more concerted national effort from the Conference of Bishops to address this problem. Second, in spite of the priest shortage, parishes should be limited in some way as to size. I know there are problems, particularly in heavily settled areas, but I feel the anger when there were scads of priests years ago and bishops (themselves mostly never in pastoral life: another deep anger) put them into all kinds of extracurricular activities rather than continually breaking up parishes into smaller communities. (As I wrote in one book, the attitude was "Any old warm body can pastor a parish." Imagine, treating the front-line initial embrace like that!) Of course, no bishop thought of the word "community" then. The word was "plant" and bigger was better—a slogan officially blessed by the monsignor reward system to those who built buildings but not necessarily community.

Whoops, my feelings are getting the better of me, so let me settle down and share with you some very practical suggestions from Father Robert Hater from his excellent article in *Church* (Winter 1988).

First, he says, center parish ministry on Jesus' teaching about the kingdom of God, a kingdom present wherever God is present and God is present in a special way with the poor and hurting. In other words, preach not the church, but the church where God's kingdom can operate and where Jesus is the absolute sign of God's caring. There are so many hurting people out there and the parish must "sell" Jesus and his personal and loving care through its ministrations.

Second, preach and teach a simple message that acknowledges and touches people's everyday lives.

Third, try to have a parish that says welcome (and in this

book I've tried to share some ideas that spell out welcome).

Fourth, develop a parish of pride, zeal, and certitude. The chapter on "Identity and Imagery" should help. Finally, I would add, both in religious education and in the Catholic schools, have a good course on the Bible and fundamentalism. Perhaps here the local parish priests could be conscripted for a short course. Better still, the diocese might invest in a few excellent teachers and pay them to travel around the diocese to the schools and parishes and give these courses.

❑ And that reminds me. Right after Vatican II, my friend, Fr. Thomas Dentici (who has since become a priest in another diocese), and I approached our bishop with the suggestion that he get a few teams who were middle-of-the-road people, but well versed in the changes and spirit of Vatican II, and have them go around the diocese giving workshops and courses so that parishes would find the transitions easier to make. We both agreed to give two years of our lives to do this. Of course, the suggestion was turned down, but I still think, over 25 years later, that it was a good idea. Get good solid people who come across well and are well versed in their field, pay them very well, and have them, with official approval, *in loco episcopi*, go around instructing and talking to small parish groups. Certainly, fundamentalism's challenges are one topic that demand serious attention.

And, finally I wonder why...

•The bishops have not funded and promoted another Bishop Sheen? I am amazed that, given the proven and durable success of the televangelists and their power (yes, even in spite of the scandals of some), we have not raised up our own for the mass media.[8]

•Creative people are not appointed to dioceses? Even the secular press has noted that Pope John Paul II has consistently been naming conservative men as bishops.[9] (I mean "creative" in the widest sense of openness and perhaps daring.)

•Bishops send scads of people away for Canon Law and almost no one for the arts?

•Dioceses are not made smaller? I feel sorry for the bishops who are already overburdened, play many roles, and have to cover territories that are not only large but diverse. How can you get to know your people—and vice versa? In the early centuries of our church there were many, many dioceses, and since it is an axiom (I just made it up) that a man can be twice the bishop with half the number of people, we should split dioceses (yes, consolidate the diocesan papers and perhaps even finances) and even have a limited number of people who can shepherd since parishes ought to have a limited number of families.

As the musical King of Siam sang, "Is a puzzlement!"

Afterword

I suppose most of us at one time or another gets the Aquinas feeling. If the story is true that at the end of his life Thomas felt that all his multitudinous writing were but "straw," that means he had a new, a different, experience of life and God that shook his perspective like a sharp, sudden wind that slams a silent shutter. A new dimension takes hold that scatters pride, lays low assumptions, and opens wide a new vision—something like an intellectual falling in love.

I have these momentary feelings when I read powerful books like Niall O'Brien's *Revolution from the Heart* or Dominique Lapierre's *City of Joy*. Such stories challenge what has been written here and offer prophetic depths and commentaries that make one's efforts look self-serving indeed. Happily, the moment passes, and I console myself that I was obviously not meant to go to the Philippines or India, whose names in my early years meant little or nothing to me. What God has wanted, apparently, was that I would be in mainstream American parish life, in middle- to upper-class parish life at that. The slums, the alley ways, the heavily ethnic have not been my steady fare. Of course, I have no apology for this. (Who am I to question God?) I mention it only to remind myself—and the reader—that there are other experiences, other ways to be church, other gifts flourishing in the most unlikely places and that knowing this helps us keep our perspective about our own experiences.

On the other hand, I remind myself (and the reader) as well that, if there's a lot of prophetic goings-on in exotic places, there's a lot of good, a lot of life-givingness going on in the mainstream parishes where we are planted, that God is "Emmanuel" there too, that the parishes we know can be wonderful communities full of shared and collaborative ministries, epiphanies scattered throughout our land; that they, durable and flexible as they are, truly are worth preserving, worth getting one's "hands-on." I also remind myself and others that in our better moments, for all of our mistakes and foolishness, those "hands-on" can be the hands of Christ.

Notes

CHAPTER 1

1. I am grateful for this outline to Thomas Green's book, *Come Down, Zacchaeus* (Notre Dame, IN: Ave Maria Press, 1988).
2. Pagan philosophers were much concerned with this dualism, too.
3. See Elaine Pagel's, *Adam, Eve and the Serpent* (New York: Random House, 1988), and the commentaries and reviews on it.
4. Joseph Campbell, *The Power of Myth* (New York: Doubleday, 1988), p. 53.
5. Thomas Merton, *A Vow of Conversation* (New York: Farrar, Straus, Giroux, 1988), p. 116)
6. Thomas Green, p. 49.
7. "Doing Theology: Every Believer's Task," *International Christian Digest*, September 1988, p. 9.
8. Constitution on the Church in the Modern World.
9. "Revisioning the Idea of 'Lay' Ministries" by Kathleen Walsh in the *New Blackfrairs*, November 1987, pp. 504ff.
10. John Shea, "The Christian in the World," audio tapes from ACTA Publications in conjunction with The Center for Development in Ministry, Archdiocese of Chicago, 1988.
11. See my book, *Storytelling: Imagination and Faith* (Mystic, Conn.: Twenty-Third Publications, 1984), p. 177.
12. Marge Britton, quoted in "The New American Catholic: The Challenge of Power of Responsibility," a report from The American Experience, held in Chicago, September 12-14, 1986, p. 5. Hereafter referred to as "The New American Catholic."

CHAPTER 2

1. John McDermott, "The New American Catholic," p. 5.
2. Joseph P. Sullivan, *ibid.*, p. 6.
3. *St. Anthony Messenger*, November 1988. The issue profiles novelist Walker Percy, actor Leonardo DeFillippis, and newsman Rolland Smith.
4. Eugene Kennedy, *Tomorrow's Catholics, Yesterday's Church* (New York: Harper & Row, 1988), p. 110.
5. All these are quoted from the various articles in *The New Catholic World*, May/June 1984.
6. See the summary article, "The World of the Future" by Leo Ryan in *The Tablet* (December 10, 1988).
7. See the special issue of "Spirituality and Social issues, *The Way*, 63 (Autumn 1988), and also *Social Revolution* by James E. Hug, S.J. and Rose-Marie Schershal (The Center of Concern, Washington, D.C.).
8. Dolores R. Lecky, *Laity Stirring the Church* (Philadelphia: Fortress Press, 1987), p. 77. I am indebted to her for some of the suggestions here. Anything she writes is worth reading. See, for example, her article, "The Experience of God in Everyday Life" in *The Way*, 60 (Autumn 1987), p. 12ff.

9. Gregory F. Augustine Pierce, "A Spirituality of Work" in *Praying*, a bimonthly of the *National Catholic Reporter*, No. 26. See also Archbishop John Roach's pastoral, "A Friendship Unlimited."

10. Thomas Groome, "Signs of Hope" in PACE (12, 1981), p. 3. See also the critically acclaimed book, *The Papacy and the Church: A Study of Praxis and Reception in Ecclesiastical Perspective* by Robert E. Dionne, S.M.

11. "The New American Catholic," p. 8. For work being done on marketplace spirituality and the place of the laity consult PILLAR, the Pallotine Institute for Lay Leadership and Apostolate Research based at Seton Hall University, South Orange, N.J., it describes itself as "a Catholic center for research and formation on the vocation and mission of the laity in Church and society." See also the 3-part series of paperbacks by Arthur Baranowski, "Called to Be Church" on how the parish can form the basis for small Christian communities. From St. Anthony Messenger Press, 1615 Republic Street, Cincinnati, Ohio 45210.

12. Quoted in Margaret Brennan's fine article, "In the End the Lion Is God," *The Way* (January 1988), p. 11. For an excellent article on God's image see Carolyn Osiek's article, "Images of God: Breaking Boundaries" in *Spirituality Today*, Winter 1988, p. 333ff.

13. For workshops on the Parish Cell System, contact St. Boniface Church, 8330 Johnson Street, Pembroke Pines, Florida 33024. Phone (305) 432-2750.

CHAPTER 3

1. *National Geographic* magazine, December 1988, p. 767. The whole end of the year (1988) issue is devoted to the planet earth.

2. *Ibid.*, p. 938.

3. Tom Wolfe, "The 21st Century Limited," *The Boston Globe* (January 17, 1988, p. A37.

4. I am indebted to Father Joseph Nolan for pulling together these comments in his "Good News" homily notes (December 11, 1988).

5. 47?

6. Paul D. Robbins, "Must Men Be Friendless?" in *Leadership* (Fall Quarter, 1988), p. 24ff.

7. Paul Schurman, Th.D., "Male Liberation," *Pastoral Psychology* (Spring 1987), p. 192.

CHAPTER 4

1. Avery Dulles, "Catholicity and Catholicism in *Theology Digest* (Fall 1987), p. 203.

2. Ed Marciniak, a January 31, 1987, address at St. Thomas University in Miami, Florida, appearing also in *American & Catholic: The New Debate* (South Orange, N.J.: Pillar Books), p. 64.

3. *Ibid.*

4. David N. Power, "Evolution of the Priesthood" in *Church* magazine (Fall 1988), p. 21.

5. Casey Bailey, S.J. "Living as a Christian in Hindu, Buddhist Culture," *Maryknoll* magazine (January 1989), p. 10.

CHAPTER 5

1. Eugene Kennedy, *op, cit.*, p. 18.
2. *The National Catholic Reporter*, September 11, 1987, p. 8.
3. *America* magazine, August 1-8, 1987, p. 54.

CHAPTER 7

1. I am grateful to Dr. Donald Lozier of the Archdiocese of Milwaukee for this summary in the area of change and the future.
2. Joseph Champlin, "Welcoming Marginal Catholics" in *Church* (Spring 1989, p. 8). See his book, *The Marginal Catholic: Challenge, Don't Crush* (Ave Maria, 1989). See also "Who Is a True Catholic? Social Boundaries on the Church" by David C. Leege, Notre Dame Study of Catholic Parish Life (Report No. 12), March 1988.

CHAPTER 10

1. Edward Wakin, "What's the Church Doing for Catholic Singles?" *Our Sunday Visitor* (September 4, 1988), p. 122-123. See also, "Where Are the Young Adults?" by Carol A. Gura in *Catholic Evangelization* (May/June 1988), p. 14ff.

CHAPTER 11

1. Quoted in "The Road to Emmaus" column by Lou Jacquet, *Our Sunday Visitor* (June 5, 1988), p. 23.
2. Robert Bellah, "The Church as the Context for the Family" in *New Oxford Review* (December 1997), p. 7.
3. See, for example, my book *Becoming a Man: Basic Information, Guidance and Attitudes on Sex for Boys* (Mystic, Conn.: Twenty-Third Publications, 1988); *Sex Respect: The Option of True Sexual Freedom* by Coleen Kelly Mast (Bradley, Ill.: Respect, Inc. and *Why Wait?* by Josh McDowell (San Bernardino, Cal.: Here's Life Publishers.

CHAPTER 14

1. Letter to the editor, *The Tablet* (October 22, 1988), p. 1211.
2. See Andrew Greeley, "Where Have All the Contributions Gone? And Why?, *National Catholic Reporter* (November 11, 1988), p. 17.

CHAPTER 15

1. Quoted by Tim Unsworth in "Where Are the Priests?" in *Notre Dame* magazine (Autumn 1988).
2. *Ibid.* See also the data from Cara (Center for Applied Research in the Apostolate) based at 3700 Oakview Terrace, NE, Washington, D.C. 20017; also see *Future of Catholic Leadership: Responses to the Priest Shortage* by Dean Hoge (Sheed & Ward). Bishop Unterkoefler of Charleston, S.C., has announced plans to establish a special institute "to train leaders of worship for those occasions when a priest is not available for Sunday Mass."

3. Address to the Canadian Bishops at the Vatican, *Origins*, November 24, 1988.

4. Patti Jane Pelton, pastoral associate at St. Francis Xavier in Chicago, quoted in *Update* (October-November 1988), p. 14.

5. Quoted in *National Catholic Reporter* (November 1988), p.

6. Letters to the Editor, *Commonweal* (December 2, 1988), p. 642.

7. Karl Rahner, *Theological Investigations*, Volume XIX (New York: Crossroad, , 1983), p. 71 and 79ff.

8. David N. Power, *op. cit.*, p. 17.

9. See the articles and response of Roman Cholij in the November 1988 and February 1989 issues of *Priests and People*. Also Daniel Callam, C.S.B., "The Origins of Clerical Celibacy" (Oxford University, 1977 and in *Theological Studies*, 1980 and 1984).

10. William McCready in *Update* (Association of Chicago Priests, December 1988-January 1989), p. 6.

11. *Commonweal, op. cit.,* p. 668.

12. Charles Dickson, "A Protestant Minister Looks at Catholics" in *Catholic Digest* (September 1988), p. 94.

13. For a creative attempt to come to terms with this issue, see Bishop Raymond Lucker's report on consolidating parishes. Send to: Diocese of New Ulm, 1400 Chancery Lane, New Ulm, MN 56073.

14. For a new approach to ministry formation see the work spearheaded by moral theologian Rev. Timothy O'Connell, Director of the Institute of Pastoral Studies, Loyola University of Chicago. See the newsletter, *Parish Ministry Link*, from the Institute for Pastoral Life, 2015 East 72nd Street, Kansas City, MO 64132, November-December 1988.

CHAPTER 16

1. William McCready quoted in Eugene Kennedy, p. 40.

2. Richard Rohr, "Masculine Spirituality," a reprint from *Praying*, a publication of the National Catholic Reporter.

3. "From Revival Tent to Mainstream" in *U.S. News and World Report* (December 19, 1988), p. 61. Three good books to consult are: *Bible Believers: Fundamentalists in the Modern World* by Tatom Ammerman (New Brunswick, N.J.: Rutgers Univ. Press, 1987), *Keeping Them Out of the Hands of Satan* by Susan D. Rose (New York: Routledge, 1988), and for Catholic polemics, *Catholics and Fundamentalism* by Karl Keating (San Francisco: Ignatius Press, 1988).

4. David Blanchard, "Hispanic Pastoral Life" in *Church* (Fall 1988), p. 22. Needless to say, the commercial world is noticing them. "If you want a big, new market, try reaching U.S. Hispanics. They're 19 million strong, with $130 billion to spend." (*Fortune*).

5. "Priesthood, Ministry, and Religious Life: Some Historical and Historiographical Considerations" by John W. O'Malley, *Theological Studies* (June 1988), p. 251. This whole article is intriguing.

6. *Ibid.*, p. 256. See also the very informative article, "The Local Church in the West (1500-1945)" by Giuseppe Alberigo, *Heythrope Journal* (1987), pp. 125-143.

7. One of the best books to read on this whole question is Ladislas

Orsy's *The Church: Learning and Teaching* (Wilmington, DE: Michael Glazier, Inc., 1987).

8. A notable insight argues that "if one agrees that theology is a statement about life and tackles the ultimate meaning in life, then television is theology." Therefore, all the more to have some command of it rather than react to it. See "The Church's Response to the Media: Twenty-Five Years After *Inter Mirifica*," by Robert P. Wasnak, *America* (January 21, 1989), pp. 36ff.

9. See, for example, *Time* magazine (January 16, 1989, p. 62). It is worth remembering that the papacy gained control of appointing bishops only several centuries ago; and even then, such power of appointment was not universal and was always subject to some limitation. Today papal appointment of bishops is both universal and without limits. Before that, bishops were elected by the local clergy and laity and at times the civil power (whose patronage system had its abuses too).

APPENDIX

CENSUS FORMS

Census Taker _____

       Name   Phone

St. Mary's Parish
Colts Neck, N.J.

Perhaps its best to start off with the sensitive issue of locating your status in the parish. Two reasons for this, especially for anyone in "D" category, are: (1) There are so many families that wish to join us from outside the parish boundaries that we could make room for if we knew for sure that some families in the parish no longer wished to be identified with it. (2) It might give us the chance, if so desired, to dialogue and renew ourselves with those who may have drifted for some reason or other.

So, please check off one of the categories below. If you check the first three, then proceed to fill out the Census Form on the other side.

____ A. I (we) am a registered parishioner and desire to continue as such. We attend church worship every weekend.

____ B. I (we) am a registered parishioner and desire to continue as such even though I (we) do not attend church worship every weekend.

____ C. I (we) am a registered parishioner, but no longer go to church at all. I (we) wish, however, to continue to remain on the parish files and mailing list.

If you wish, would you explain why you no longer attend church?

_____

_____

____D. I (we) am a registered parishioner, but do not bother with church anymore. I (we) wish to be removed from the parish register, files, and mailing list.

_____

If you wish, would you explain why? _____

_____

_____

Name_____

Address_____

___ E. I (we) am not registered in the parish and never have been. However, I would like to register here and now with this census form.

NOTE: "E" does not automatically register you. Fill out the other side, but acceptance of the form will be determined by the pastor.

Census Taker_____ Today's Date _____
St. Mary's Parish Census
Colts Neck, N.J.

Full Name_____ Phone No. _____

Mailing Address _____

_____

Occupation_____

Birthdate _____
(Month, Date, Year)

Status;

_Single __ Married (if Wife, Insert Maiden Name Here

_Widowed __ Separated _Divorced & Single _ Divorced & Remarried

Religion___ Baptized___ First Communion___ Confirmed ___

Attend Mass: ___ Regularly ___ Occasionally ___Never

If Married;

Was Your Marriage Witnessed By A Catholic Priest? __ Yes __No

Husband's (or Wife's Maiden)

Name_____

Occupation_____ Birthdate_____

Religion ___ Baptized ___ First Communion___ Confirmed ___

Attend Mass: ___ Regularly ___ Occasionally ___ Never

Children 18 & Under Including Those Away From School. Over 18 Fill Out
Own Form.

Name Birthdate Rel. Baptized 1st Comm. Conf. School Grade

_____

_____

_____

Other Parishioners, Relatives, Boarders Living With You. (Indicate with note
whether any of these is disabled, a shut-in or ill.)

Name Birthdate Rel. Baptized 1st Comm. Conf. Relationship

_____

_____

_____

SECTION I

This questionnaire is anonymous (no names please) so that you can respond
as honestly as you can. Put a check mark next to the one (and only one) statement that best reflects how you feel. You'll notice that there are three sets of
the same statements marked Person A, Person B, and Person C. This is so that
at least three people in your house can also express their opinions if they care
to. Your census taker will pick up this questionnaire also—unless you prefer
to mail it in.

1. I find most meaning in attending Mass at:

Person A	Person B	Person C
___St. Mary's	___St. Mary's	___St. Mary's
___another local church	___another local church	___another local church
___a local chapel or college campus	___a local chapel or college campus	___a local chapel or college campus
___a church in another town	___a church in another town	___a church in another town

2. At Mass I most prefer:

Person A	Person B	Person C
___no music	___no music	___no music
___only organ music	___only organ music	___only organ music
___the choir singing	___the choir singing	___the choir singing
___folk music	___folk music	___ folk music
___congregational singing	___congregational singing	___congregational singing

3. I would most prefer to learn about my faith by:

Person A	Person B	Person C
___ reading more about it	___reading more about it	___reading more about it
___through a sermon	___through a sermon	___through a sermon
___attending parish lectures	___attending parish lectures	___attending parish lectures
___discussion group	___discussion groups	___discussion groups

4. The last time I talked with my parish priest in person or over the phone was:

Person A	Person B	Person C
___in the past 2 days	___in the past 2 days	___in the past 2 days
___in the past week	___in the past week	___in the past week
___in the past month	___in the past month	___in the past month
___in the past 6 months	___in the past 6 months	___in the past 6 months
___in the past 5 or more years	___in the past 5 or more years	___in the past 5 or more years
___never	___never	___never

5. The last time I went to Communion was:

Person A	Person B	Person C
___in the past week	___in the past week	___in the past week
___in the past month	___in the past month	___in the past month
___in the past 6 months	___in the past 6 months	___in the past 6 months
___in the past 12 months	___in the past 12 months	___in the past 12 months
___in the past 5 years	___in the past 5 years	___in the past 5 years
___more than 5 years ago	___more than 5 years ago	___more than 5 years ago

6. The last time I went to Confession (private or communal — circle one) was:

___in the past week	___in the past week	___in the past week
___in the past month	___in the past month	___in the past month
___in the past 6 months	___in the past 6 months	___in the past 6 months
___in the past 12 months	___in the past 12 months	___in the past 12 months
___in the past 5 years	___in the past 5 years	___in the past 5 years
___ more than 5 years ago	___more than 5 years ago	___more than 5 years ago

7. Being a Roman Catholic in today's times is:

Person A	Person B	Person C
___extremely dificult	___extremely difficult	___extremely difficult
___very difficult	___very difficult	___very difficult
___difficult but worth it	___difficult but worth it	___difficult but worth it
___easy	___easy	___easy
___very easy	___very easy	___very easy

8. My feeling about St. Mary's Parish is:

Person A	Person B	Person C
___very good	___very good	___very good
___good	___good	___good
___fair	___fair	___fair
___poor	___poor	___poor
___indifferent	___indifferent	___indifferent

9. The sermons given by Father Mokrzycki at St. Mary's are generally:

Person A	Person B	Person C
___very good	___very good	___very good
___good	___good	___good
___fair	___fair	___fair
___poor	___poor	___poor
___ indifferent	___indifferent	___indifferent

10. The sermons given by Father Williams at St. Mary's are generally:

Person A	Person B	Person C
___very good	___very good	___very good
___good	___good	___good

___fair	___fair	___fair
___poor	___poor	___poor
___indifferent	___indifferent	___indifferent

11. The sermons given by Father Bausch at St. Mary's are generally:

Person A	Person B	Person C
___very good	___very good	___very good
___good	___good	___good
___fair	___fair	___fair
___poor	___poor	___poor
___indifferent	___indifferent	___indifferent

12. The music at Mass (cantors, organists, congregational singing) is generally:

Person A	Person B	Person C
___very good	___very good	___very good
___good	___good	___good
___fair	___fair	___fair
___poor	___poor	___poor
___indifferent	___indifferent	___indifferent

13. The lectors are generally:

Person A	Person B	Person C
___very good	___very good	___very good
___good	___good	___good
___fair	___fair	___fair
___poor	___poor	___poor
___indifferent	___indifferent	___indifferent

14. The Parish CCD program is generally:

Person A	Person B	Person C
___very good	___very good	___very good
___good	___good	___good
___fair	___fair	___fair
___poor	___poor	___poor
___indifferent	___indifferent	___indifferent

15. The banners, flowers, decorations for special feasts and occasions are generally:

Person A	Person B	Person C
__very good	__very good	__very good
__good	__good	__good
__fair	__fair	__fair
__poor	__poor	__poor
__indifferent	__indifferent	__indifferent

16. The Parish Organizations (the Rosary Guild and Men's Guild) are generally:

Person A	Person B	Person C
__very good	__very good	__very good
__good	__good	__good
__fair	__fair	__fair
__poor	__poor	__poor
__indifferent	__indifferent	__indifferent

17. I believe in:

a) A Personal God

__yes   __no   __unsure

b) Jesus as divine Son of God

__yes   __no   __unsure

c) Heaven

__yes   __no   __unsure

d) Sacraments as occasions of union with God

__yes   __no   __unsure

e) God's assistance is available

__yes   __no   __unsure

f) Jesus' resurrection

__yes   __no   __unsure

g) Existence of hell

__yes   __no   __unsure

h) Our redemption through Christ

__yes   __no   __unsure

i) the Church as a community of believers

__yes   __no   __unsure

218 / THE HANDS-ON PARISH

18. I have thoughts of agreement or disagreement with the following:

a) responsibility to share with those who have less

___agree   ___disagree

b) responsibility to oppose injustice

___agree   ___disagree

c) moral convictions affect work

___agree   ___disagree

d) Church rules are no longer clear

___agree   ___disagree

e) Confused about Church's teachings

___agree   ___disagree

f) Church's rules are too inflexible

___agree   ___disagree

And now, if you will, just a few fill-ins (where they apply). Other household members can copy these statements on another piece of paper and attach them to this if they wish.

19. Something I've always wanted to say to the pastor is this:

_____

_____

_____

_____

20. What do you think of the pastor?

_____

_____

_____

_____

21. What do you think of the Associate Pastor? (Sister Claire?)

_____

_____

_____

_____

22. If you marked any of the preceding pages as only fair, poor or indifferent, can you give suggestions for improvement? (Identify areas)

_____

_____

_____

_____

23. I think the parish should:

_____

_____

_____

_____

24. I think the biggest problem we the people have to face today is:

_____

_____

_____

_____

25. Something we never hear preached from the pulpit—which we should hear—is:

_____

_____

_____

26. Given the rising cost of construction and the cost of energy, do you think we should reconsider the erection of a Parish Center?

_____yes   _____no

27. Any other comments?

_____

_____

_____

Parish Resources

For copies of anything that might interest you, write to St. Mary's Parish, Highway 34, Colts Neck, N.J. 07722. You may also call: 1-201-780-2666. We will charge you only what it costs us to print and mail. Make checks payable to "St. Mary's Church."

A copy of the annual parish booklet $5.00
A copy of the Covenant $2.00
A packet of six booklets $15.00

If interested in coming to a Hands-On workshop at St. Mary's—given during the summer from Monday evenings to Friday mornings—write to "Workshop" in care of St. Mary's.

If interested in just a visit, write to "Hospitality" in care of St. Mary's.

If interested in just one segment, for example, the Lazarus or the One-on-One ministries, write to that title in care of St. Mary's.